Hip to the Trip

HIP TO THE TRIP

A CULTURAL
HISTORY OF ROUTE 66

Peter B. Dedek

UNIVERSITY OF NEW MEXICO PRESS ALBUQUERQUE

Library of Congress Cataloging-in-Publication Data

Dedek, Peter B., 1964–

Hip to the trip : a cultural history of Route 66 / Peter B. Dedek.

p. cm.

Includes bibliographical references and index.

ISBN 978-0-8263-4194-5 (pbk. : alk. paper)

1. United States Highway 66—History.

2. Express highways—Social aspects—United States.

3. Cultural landscapes—United States.

I. Title.

HE356.U55D43 2007

388.1'220973—dc22

2006039622

Design and composition: Melissa Tandysh

I'd like to thank Andrew Gulliford,
Loren McWatters, Will Gray, and
Sharon Vaughan for their support and help
with the creation of this book.

Contents

List of Illustrations

Illustrations:

Introduction

Why Route 66?

You're all packed up and on your way. Your vacation, a long-waited auto trip to California, has finally begun. Just south of Chicago, the kids giggle with anticipation as you turn your shiny new '57 Chevy onto the main road. Sleek signs with flashy neon logos line the busy suburban highway. You drive through the congested suburbs, eager to get out into the country.

Farther south, the two-lane highway guides your two glistening rocketlike hood ornaments straight into the flat prairie horizon. Nothing's ahead except open fields and happy anticipation as you race past a familiar black-and-white Route 66 shield. You're going to see the whole road this time, all the way to the Santa Monica Pier.

Several hours into your drive, you stop at a lonely gas station, a "Phillips 66," which looks like a small European cottage, to gas up. You take out and unfold a map of the United States as the uniformed gas attendant fills your tank, cleans your windshield, and checks your oil. A red line marked "Route 66" will lead you all the way to California. You will first go past the green, flat prairies of southern Illinois and travel through the gently rolling hills of Missouri's Ozarks and across the farmlands of Kansas and eastern Oklahoma. Then you will drive west toward the 100th meridian and witness the vast, hazel, high plains of western Oklahoma and Texas, the arid buttes and scattered Indian ruins of New Mexico, the snow-covered mountains and desiccated deserts of Arizona. Finally you will pass Death Valley, the starkest landscape of all, and cross over the cactus-covered mountains to the verdant orange groves and sunny beaches of southern California. Along the way, you hope to stop at all of the snake pits, souvenir shops, Indian trading posts, and Indian ruins that you can stand, eat mounds of hearty American food at roadside cafes, and stay at remote motels with exotic names like the De Anza and the Wigwam Village. With everyone back in the car, you start your engine and begin your fascinating journey west.

My first encounter with "Route 66" was nothing like this. It took place in the early 1990s as I was traveling on the beltway just west of Washington, D. C., and took an interstate highway west toward Winchester, Virginia. Next to the wide shoulder of that generic highway I spotted a red, white, and blue highway shield that read "Interstate 66." I asked myself "is this *the* Route 66?" But even as the words left my lips, I realized, perhaps by intuition, that this sterile four-lane monster leading west into the hills of northern Virginia could not be *the* Route 66. "Wasn't Route 66 in the West?" I said, "and wasn't it big in the 1950s?" This encounter—and the resulting effort to find out what Route 66 actually *was* and why it is so famous—lead to my first journey down the actual "Mother Road" and eventually to my writing this book.

Virtually every American has heard of "Route 66" or technically, "U.S. Highway 66," and some have a vague notion, like I did in 1992, that the highway was somehow "western" and a thing of the past, but that's about all they usually can say about it. Route 66 is well known but not widely understood. However, a growing number of visitors from all over the world are becoming very familiar with and enamored of the highway. They associate the route with a variety of images, ideas, and nostalgic experiences, real or imagined, such as the scene I described at the beginning of this chapter.

U.S. Highway 66 has two histories: a material one as a major U.S. transportation corridor from 1926 to about 1970 and a symbolic one as a pillar of mid-twentieth-century American automobile culture and tourism. While not the longest or the first long-distance highway across the United States (the Lincoln Highway from New York City to

San Francisco was first), Route 66 enjoys a unique place in American popular culture because, unlike most other preinterstate U.S. highways, it has earned a distinct and widespread popular identity. Before its official closure in 1985, historic U.S. 66 had long been associated with the deserts, Indians, and cowboys of the Southwest, the "Okies" of the Great Depression, and with the millions of vacationers who took to the highway in their streamlined automobiles and found adventure on the open road from the late 1940s until the 1970s. The highway has maintained these associations since it was closed.

There are few, if any, television commercials that mention U.S. Highway 40 or U.S. Highway 30, both of which were heavily traveled truly coast-to-coast historic highways (Route 66 linked Chicago and Los Angeles). Yet Route 66 has such name recognition that in the past twenty years, it has been used to advertise products ranging from blue jeans, to root beer, to automobiles. Like a corporation that uses a celebrity to endorse its brand, advertisers exploit Route 66's notoriety to sell products both on and off the road. As one Arizona merchant put it, "If something has the [Route 66] shield on it, it will sell."[1]

Route 66's path to fame began in the late nineteenth century with the advertising campaigns of the Atchison, Topeka, & Santa Fe (AT&SF) and the Southern Pacific Railroads. These railroads ran passenger trains along tracks that roughly paralleled the path Route 66 would later take (plates 1A and B). The railroads and the Fred Harvey Company, which managed hotels for the AT&SF, aggressively marketed the Southwest, mostly using the Pueblo Indians and the myth of the Old West to entice potential tourists from the East to visit this previously wild and inhospitable region.[2] In addition to featuring the Pueblo Indians, railroad advertisements occasionally also featured Plains Indians such as the Apache as well as cowboys and Mexican Americans, often using clichéd representations of their regalia, cultural activities, ceremonies, and architecture.

Millions of tourists saw the Southwest by train from the 1880s to the 1940s. However, soon after its official designation in 1926, Route 66 became the primary auto and truck route between Chicago and Los Angeles and began to replace the railroads as the primary mode of tourist travel. Initially, many motorists and truckers chose U.S. 66 rather than other long-distance highways because the highway took the shortest feasible route directly from the Midwest to southern California and was more passable in winter than other highways, such as U.S. 30.[3] As motorists followed its diagonal path across the western half of the continent, Route 66 took them through the Southwest, a region already made popular by the railroads. By 1930, many Americans were using the highway as a tourist route to see natural wonders such as the Grand Canyon, the Painted Desert, and the Petrified Forest and to access cultural sights such as Anasazi ruins, Hopi pueblos, and the city of Santa Fe, dubbed "America's oldest capital."[4] People drove Route 66 to see the same sights that their parents had seen by train.

With Route 66 as the primary automobile route through the Southwest, previously established regional images eventually became associated with the highway itself, and the highway gained fame as the best route to and through the Wild West, where the auto tourist would encounter the Indian, the frontier, and the open road.

The realities that tourists encountered along Route 66 often differed from the images promoted in the travel literature produced by railroads, regional boosters, and highway organizations. Instead of coming into contact with authentic Native American cultures and the untamed wilderness of the Wild West, motorists experienced the West in the form of cafés shaped like giant sombreros, faux adobe motels designed to mimic ancient pueblos or haciendas, and souvenirs sold at phony Indian trading posts and snake pits. Despite this artificial quality, these travel experiences seem to inspire much of the current nostalgia for Route 66. Neon road signs featuring "wild" Indians in feathered headdresses or cowboys in ten-gallon hats twirling lassos and thematic commercial architecture featuring faux adobe stucco walls adorned with nonfunctioning vigas and *canles* or concrete cones painted up to look like Indian teepees had more impact on the immediate roadside landscape than did authentic cultural landmarks, which were often located in inconvenient places a distance from the highway.

Tourist establishments, such as Frontier City near Oklahoma City, attempted to recreate Hollywood's version of the "Wild West" for paying visitors. Roadside retailers and motel operators adapted, refined, and often abstracted the images originally created by the railroads for use on Route 66. Mom-and-pop "tourist traps," such as Ed Galloway's Totem Pole Park near Foyil, Oklahoma, defined the Route 66 experience.[5]

Although the highway enjoyed only about thirty years of dominance—from 1926 to around 1956—as a primary auto and truck route, after which it underwent a period of gradual decline that lasted into the 1980s as it was replaced by interstates, Route 66 became forever fixed in the history and lore of the Southwest and the United States as a whole. Popular culture, such as John Steinbeck's 1939 novel, *The Grapes of Wrath*, Bobby Troup's 1946 lyrics, "Get Your Kicks on Route 66," and the 1960–64 television show, *Route 66*, helped to immortalize the highway. With names such as the "Mother Road," the "Main Street of America," and the "Will Rogers Highway," Route 66 became the most famous road in America.

Despite the popularity that Route 66 had achieved by the time a total of five new interstate highways replaced its two-lane segments, most motorists gladly left the old pavement and put its congestion and dangerous curves behind them. Many observers in the 1970s and early 1980s thought that Route 66 was dead.[6] This sentiment must have been shared by the highway officials who designated the short interstate highway west of Washington, D.C., as "Interstate 66" without any regard or respect for the famous U.S. Highway 66. It wasn't until interstates completely bypassed Route 66 in 1984 that a new breed of road enthusiasts began to form organizations dedicated to preserving the memory of the old road.

By this time, Route 66 had come to represent the eras in which it was active, particularly the 1930s and the 1950s, and continued to symbolize concepts such as the Old West (as personified by the cowboy and the Indian), flight from adversity (as personified by the "Okie"), and the power and freedom of the private automobile (represented by the sleek cars of the 1950s). Marketing, literature, songs, and television reinforced Route 66 images. The ten half-buried cars of the Cadillac Ranch near Amarillo, Texas; the lonely ruins of gas stations, "Indian" trading posts, and motels along the vacant ghost road; the sad yet heroic faces of Dust Bowl migrants; and streamlined 1950s "sleds" roaring across the arid West all help to give Route 66 its unique identity. For many, Route 66 also inspires ideas of freedom and mobility as well as the innocence of youth.

Route 66 means different things to different people. To some contemporary enthusiasts, the highway is a symbol and remnant of the "good old days" of the 1950s, which they believe was a moral and upstanding period of American history. For others, the highway represents the beginnings of the freewheeling road culture of individuals such as Jack Kerouac, who helped spawn the cultural changes of the 1960s. Others see Route 66 primarily as the road of migration and "flight" of the Okies and, later, of GIs returning from the Second World War looking for a new life in California. To most Americans, Route 66 represents the quintessential American highway and the route through the Southwest where the Old West lives on.

The "complexity and contradiction" (to invoke the title of Robert Venturi's tome on postmodern architecture) of historic Route 66, with its quirky neon signs, motels reminiscent of Anasazi pueblos and Spanish missions, roadside attractions adorned with strange advertising gimmicks, such as burning covered wagons, giant kachina dolls, and twenty-foot-high arrows, have retained their appeal with the citizens of the postmodern world. When compared to the functional purity of the interstate highways, which were the product of the modernist mentality of the 1950s, Route 66 stands out as a fascinating spectacle. Unlike interstates, which separate motorists from the landscape, Route 66 followed the curves of the landscape and brought motorists in direct contact with unusual roadside businesses, genuine historic structures, and famous natural monuments where they could stop at will. Many current historic Route 66 tourists want to share the relative intimacy with the landscape that motorists enjoyed in the past.

Thousands of Route 66 enthusiasts, including people who do not reside on or near the road, currently belong to preservation and promotional organizations for the highway. Each of the eight Route 66 states—Illinois, Missouri, Kansas, Oklahoma, Texas, New Mexico, Arizona, and California—have an active grassroots preservation organization dedicated to saving and interpreting the highway. In addition, enthusiasts have founded the national *Route 66 Magazine* and several other specialty publications, created hundreds of Internet sites dedicated to Route 66, formed a National Route 66 Federation, and established international Route 66 organizations in Europe, Canada, and Japan. Numerous museums and visitors centers dedicated to Route 66 line the old road, including two museums located in Elk City and Clinton, Oklahoma (cities that are only thirty miles apart). In addition to the museums and visitor centers, guided bus tours, drive-a-thons, motorcycle rallies, and convoys of vintage recreational vehicles travel the route on a regular basis. The highway's fans help generate untold tourist dollars for Route 66 communities.[7] This enthusiasm also resulted in the passage of a major federal historic preservation initiative, the Route 66 Corridor Act of 1999.

In the past twenty or so years, media attention has fueled renewed interest in Route 66. American and European magazines, including *National Geographic, Newsweek,* and *Der Spiegel,* and television producers, such as the Travel Channel and Public Broadcasting System, have produced stories on Route 66.[8]

Thousands of foreigners, especially Germans, Swiss, and Japanese, come to remote sites in Arizona, New Mexico, and Oklahoma to tour Route 66. One German tourist said he came to see the "real America." By this, he meant the America of western literature and John Steinbeck, not the America of chain motels and franchised fast food restaurants. Another German visitor to Seligman, Arizona, summed up the view of many foreign visitors when he said, "If you build a McDonald's here, we will stop coming."[9]

Along with its appeal for tourists, Route 66 has deep significance for Americans who have spent their lives driving it. A Route 66 enthusiast in Illinois, who has lived and worked on Route 66 for over fifty years, describes the highway as "an adventure."[10] A longtime gas station operator on the highway in central Illinois refers to Route 66 as "our history."[11] Michael Taylor, director of the federal Route 66 Corridor Preservation Program, describes Route 66 as the "open road, a two-laner that hugs the landscape."[12] Others, such as author Michael Wallis who wrote *Route 66: The Mother Road,* a widely read tribute to the highway, characterize Route 66 as "a metaphor for the way the United States used to be—real family values without the buzz words."[13]

Although Route 66 survives today more as a symbol than as an actual highway, thousands of historic sites do survive along the various alignments of old Route 66, particularly west of Missouri. A number of these historic resources, such as the U-Drop Inn in Shamrock, Texas, and the Will Rogers Hotel in Claremore, Oklahoma, are successful examples of preservation; others, such as the Coral Courts Motel in St. Louis, Missouri, and the Club Cafe in Santa Rosa, New Mexico, have vanished.

Today, the remaining segments of Route 66 offer an intimate view of many of the same roadside businesses, historic structures, and natural monuments that our parents and grandparents experienced. Although many historic sites along the highway are currently threatened, isolated roadside architecture and ruins, remote towns, historic cityscapes, and diverse natural areas still enhance Route 66.

In some cases, the decay of the eclectic structures and buildings along Route 66 is part of their attractiveness.

Much of the appeal of Route 66 lies in its sense of authenticity and place. While the symbols of the road, such as the shield, have been widely marketed, the road itself has yet to be packaged. One can still travel the often-lonely stretches of road and walk among the ruins, meet genuine Route 66 personalities, stay in the same motels, and eat at the same restaurants, sometimes run by the same families, as the original tourists. Route 66 represents a linear community that is truly "of the people, by the people, for the people." The surviving segments comprise an American ruin. Europe has castles, cathedrals, and Roman aqueducts: the United States has tourist courts, gas stations, and vintage highway viaducts.

Today, historic Route 66 presents visitors with a jumble of popular cultural images and icons, many involving the automobile and the Southwest, which developed over more than a century. While traveling the route, the contemporary traveler encounters images and architecture from various periods and ruins that reflect multiple layers of memory, history, and myth. Motorists take in authentic Indian and Spanish colonial sites and artifacts alongside the ruins of the motels, cafes, and tourist traps that tried to imitate them. On Route 66, the artificial joins the authentic, creating a cultural and natural collage that stretches from prehistory to the present.

Because of its association with the Southwest and its popularity with Americans, Route 66 provides a unique vantage point from which to better understand American popular culture from the 1920s to the present. Route 66 has such notoriety and such a rich array of images, concepts, and metaphors associated with it that studying its place in American culture reveals a great deal about how Americans view, revere, and revile the recent past.

The purpose of this book is not to simply recount the history of Route 66 but to create a comprehensive portrait of the cultural meaning of the highway that explores what Route 66 was, what it is today, and what it may become in the future.

CHAPTER ONE

"Wild" Lands and "Tamed" Indians
Cultural Stereotypes and Route 66

Stereotypes helped make Route 66 famous. From the 1920s on, images of Native Americans as feathered Indian chiefs, cowboys as clean-cut Anglo-Saxon heroes, and Mexicans as colorful dons and feisty señoritas appeared in Route 66 brochures and advertisements, on roadside signs, and even as roadside architecture. These ethnic stereotypes emerged from the commodification of the Southwest and its peoples by the railroads and other businesses in the late nineteenth century. As they worked to entice rail tourists to the region, the railroads exploited and distorted the area's rich cultures and history.

When the Atchison, Topeka, and Santa Fe Railway (AT&SF) entered the Southwest around 1880, it often built its tracks alongside earlier wagon roads and footpaths. At first, the railroads ignored local history and cultures, being focused primarily on transporting people and goods across the deserts and mountains to California. It wasn't until the mid 1890s that the western railroads realized the potential that the area had for tourism and began to study and promote the area's Indian and Spanish heritage.[1]

Railroad promoters found that the landscapes, cultures, and history of the region through which Route 66 would later pass were rich and varied. Around the turn of the century the railroads discovered that the arid land itself—its Petrified Forest, Grand Canyon, snow-capped mountains, and towering cactus—could draw tourists. The railroads also soon learned the value of Native Americans whose cultures and architecture dated back thousands of years, Spanish missionaries who arrived in the area as early as the 1500s, and the lingering stories and myths of pioneer Anglo settlers who moved into the region in the 1800s.[2]

The path that the railroads and later Route 66 followed was already well traveled by the time the rails were laid. The northeastern leg of the Route 66 corridor from Chicago, Illinois, to St. Louis, Missouri, dates back at least to the 1673 portage trail that Père Jacques Marquette and Louis Joliet blazed on their exploration of the upper Mississippi River, which followed various earlier paths blazed by Native Americans. The next leg led southwest from the Marquette and Joliet route approximated an Osage Indian trail that extended from St. Louis across Missouri to Fort Smith, Arkansas, which travelers later came to know as the "Wire Road," because the first telegraph line into the Southwest followed it.[3] The next path to the west that Route 66 would later trace was the famous Santa Fe Trail, which Pedro Vial marked out in the 1770s.[4]

In 1849 Captain Randolph Marcy and Lieutenant James Simpson led a surveying expedition to map a future "national road" across the Southwest. This road followed essentially the same path as Route 66 across Oklahoma, through the Texas panhandle, and on to Santa Fe, covering portions of the old Santa Fe Trail.[5]

In 1857 the United States Congress voted to send Lieutenant Edward Beale and his survey crew, who used camels imported from Egypt as pack animals, to plot a course west from Santa Fe along the 35th parallel, and across the Colorado River into the deserts of eastern California. The purpose of this endeavor was to improve military and civilian transportation across the southwestern frontier. This section connected with the Marcy-Simpson route, linking Fort Smith near the Arkansas River to California via a path that became known as Beale's Road.[6]

Beale's Road was the first passable wagon road through the western portion of the path that U.S. Highway 66 would eventually take. Beale predicted the future importance of the corridor when he said it would "inevitably become the great emigrant road to California."[7] From the late 1920s to the 1970s millions of migrants to California helped give Route 66 its place in American history and popular culture.

In the last two decades of the nineteenth century, rail travel rapidly superseded stagecoaches, and the time it took to travel across the Southwest decreased dramatically. Once established, the AT&SF, which dominated passenger travel in the Southwest between 1880 and 1930, and to a lesser degree the Southern Pacific Railroad, transformed the Southwest from a rugged wilderness into a tourist destination with luxurious amenities.[8]

Railroads had a dramatic impact on the landscapes along the eventual corridor of Route 66. They established the locations, basic layouts, and early architecture of most Route 66 towns. Railroad-owned land companies platted many towns on tracts of land granted by the federal government and state legislatures. These new communities became sites of railroad locomotive repair shops, freight and passenger stations, and hotels to provide passengers with a comfortable place to eat and sleep during interruptions in long train journeys. Such iconic Route 66 towns as Lincoln, Illinois; Rolla, Missouri; Gallup, New Mexico; and Kingman, Arizona, had their origins in the late nineteenth century as railroad settlements.[9] The business districts of these railroad towns were oriented toward the tracks in an easily recognizable configuration of closely spaced commercial buildings, often brick with false fronts to make them noticeable from the tracks, that defined the character of many of the many main streets through which Route 66, the "Main Street of America," would later pass. From Chicago to Los Angeles, the various alignments of Route 66 almost never lost sight of the tracks (plate 2).

Not only did the railroads transform the physical landscape, but they also altered the way tourists perceived those landscapes by giving the American Southwest a national reputation as a "land of enchantment."[10] Promotion by railroads, dime novels with western themes, and acts such as Buffalo Bill's Wild West Show provided easterners with a highly romanticized and often fictional perspective on the formerly "wild" but recently tamed Indians living in a still "untamed" southwestern landscape. Regional boosters emphasized nationalism, Anglo-Saxon ethnic pride, and an opportunity to visit segments of America that remained undeveloped.

During the railroad era, many Anglo-Americans believed that the United States was fulfilling its "manifest destiny" by taking the

Southwest and claiming hegemony over its Native American and Hispanic cultures.[11] While many white settlers tended to scorn Mexicans, they often had mixed feelings about the Native Americans, especially the Pueblo Indians.

Native Americans had fascinated Anglos since first contact, and during the romantic movement of the late eighteenth and early nineteenth centuries, philosophers invented the concept of the "noble savage." Romanticism, which emphasized emotion over reason, originated in western Europe in the mid-eighteenth century and persisted as the dominant intellectual ideology of Western society into the 1830s.[12] Rugged, dramatic scenery, peasants, lunatics, children, and "savages" fascinated the romantics. During the romantic era, Europeans began to admire mountains and wilderness areas, which most had seen as mere impediments to human progress previously. This helped create the foundation for late-nineteenth-century tourism in rugged regions such as the Southwest. Emerging as a reaction against a developing mechanized industrial civilization just as the industrial revolution was getting underway in Europe, romanticism called for a return to nature.[13]

American Indians seemed to fit perfectly into the romantic ideal of the primitive "natural man" or "noble savage" uncorrupted by Western civilization.[14] Indians came to represent the antithesis of the Protestant work ethic, affected bourgeois manners, and European social classes. The romantics' idealized notions of tribal peoples reflected little actual understanding of their cultures.[15] Sitting in European salons, romantics speculated about Native Americans and imagined that tribal peoples existed in a mythic state of perfection in complete harmony with nature.

Individuals influenced by romanticism who really did travel west and came into contact with Indians tended to represent them as mythic figures in a pastoral fantasy for the eastern and European market. Paintings by Karl Bodmer, George Catlin, and Alfred Jacob Miller from the 1830s often portrayed Indians as innocents, distant from the corrupting influences of Anglo civilization.[16]

After traveling through the American West to capture images of Plains Indians in the 1830s, artist George Catlin, for example, described Indians as "noble." He believed, however, that civilization was rapidly corrupting their cultures.[17] "Nature," he wrote "had nowhere presented more beautiful and lovely scenes than those of the vast prairies of the West" and that the "noble specimens who inhabit them—the Indian and the buffalo" were the "joint and original tenants of the soil, and fugitives together from the epoch of civilized man." Sadly, Catlin described the Indian and buffalo as being "under an equal doom," having "taken up their last abode, where their race will expire, and their bones will bleach together."

In his writings, Catlin outlined the view of tribal peoples that many tourists to the Southwest probably took—that they were "noble" but also "fugitives . . . from the epoch of civilized man."[18] Catlin had a tremendous influence on subsequent American perceptions of Native Americans and the West. He wrote a series of popular books and took his collection of paintings of Indians, sometimes bringing along living "specimens," on tours through the United States and Europe.[19]

Because of romantic depictions of Native Americans in Catlin's paintings and in other art, and a fascination with westward expansion and the West in general, the image of a Great Plains Indian in a feathered headdress became a symbol of the United States in the nineteenth century. By 1859, in an ironic twist of perception, the image of the traditional Indian had become so well associated with American nationalism and identity that the United States government replaced the small cent coin featuring a flying eagle with a new design portraying the profile of the traditional "lady liberty" that had appeared on American coins since 1793 wearing Native American full war regalia. Designed by James Barton Longacre (1794–1869), chief engraver of the United States Mint, the popular cent remained in production until 1909, when, in honor of the one hundredth anniversary of his birth, a portrait of Lincoln was chosen to replace that of the Indian.[20] The fact that American pennies and several gold coins as well proudly featured the image of a Native American at a time when the United States government was relentlessly forcing Indians onto reservations, and the Army was massacring them at places such as Sand Creek, Colorado (1864) and Wounded Knee, South Dakota (1890), illustrates the wide gulf between romantic idealism and iconography, on the one hand, and reality, on the other.

In the last three decades that the Indian head cent was in use, railroad tour brochures urged would-be travelers to see the West soon to catch a final glimpse of native cultures before they were forever lost. Cultural anthropologist Renato Rosaldo describes the desire by members of a group that perceives itself as dominant to experience the cultures and landscapes that they are in the process of destroying as "imperialist nostalgia."[21] In this instance, many Anglos assumed that although native cultures were doomed due to inevitable technological and social progress, they were worthy of study as interesting and perhaps even noble, anachronistic spectacles that should be witnessed and documented on their way to obsolescence.

Until railroads came through the Southwest in the 1870s and 1880s, few Anglo-Americans remained in the region any longer than it took to pass through to get to California, and many went to California by ship. One who did linger, novelist Washington Irving, described its arid landscapes as "desolate," "barren," "wild," and "dreary."[22] Europe remained the primary destination for American tourists. The Southwest was still difficult to access, and with the exception of migrants to California, only a few rugged pioneers and romantic wanderers, such as Catlin, made the arduous journey from the East. A few Anglos came to prospect, paint portraits of Indians, conduct business, explore, or otherwise find adventure, but never to take a relaxed holiday. At this time, native cultures held only an abstract interest for most white easterners, and before the railroads popularized southwestern Indian art and pottery through extensive marketing campaigns, Indian-made artifacts had little economic value to outsiders. Before 1880, when the AT&SF Railroad reached Albuquerque and pueblos such as Laguna on its way to California, the rural New Mexico and Arizona Indian villages existed in "feudal self-sufficiency," with their crafts serving their own practical and religious purposes.[23]

At first, most Santa Fe riders came to the region because they believed southwestern air and mineral water baths cured illnesses and generally aided health.[24] However, once they arrived in the region and traversed the arid landscape, saw Indian ruins, and visited inhabited pueblos, they often became more interested in the places they visited than the cures they had come to receive.[25] Soon, a relatively small but growing number of elite easterners began traveling west for their holidays.

To help attract additional tourists to the West, businesspeople and conservationists worked for the creation of national parks such as Yellowstone (1872) and Yosemite (1890). The Southern Pacific Railroad actively lobbied for the establishment of Yellowstone and Yosemite National Parks. Conservationist John Muir, who addressed the 1895 Sierra Club annual meeting, said, "Even the soulless Southern Pacific

R.R. Co., never counted on for anything good, helped nobly in pushing the bill for this park through Congress."[26] At the same time that the California and Wyoming national parks were drawing more tourists to the West, popularization of Indian cultures and ancient ruins of Arizona and New Mexico allowed the AT&SF and its partner, the Fred Harvey Company, to build an empire based on programmed tourism. The impact of Harvey's tours and railroad hotels became so great that Harvey garnered the title "civilizer of the West."[27]

Once they built their western lines, the AT&SF and other railroad companies flooded the East with posters, calendars, postcards, and guidebooks featuring arid western scenery to evoke sensations of mystery, adventure, and innocent romance among potential railroad travelers.[28] As early as the late 1870s, over twenty-five travel guidebooks to the West had been produced, all of which championed rail travel. The guidebooks and other railroad-sponsored promotions worked. In 1875 alone, over seventy-five thousand passengers rode the Union Pacific from Omaha, Nebraska, to San Francisco. By the end of the century, over one hundred thousand people rode trains to the West annually, bringing millions of dollars along with them.[29]

The Santa Fe Railroad did not include Indians in its advertising until the mid-1890s, in part because the railroad had continued to equip trains with Winchester rifles to protect them against Indian raids well into the 1880s. Several groups of Apaches, who staged "breakouts" from reservations and returned to their traditional homelands, often raided ranches and attacked United States soldiers.[30] Once the United States had pacified the Indians through military force and by killing off their food supply of American bison and other animals, easterners could more easily consider Native Americans as potent symbol of child-like freedom and vanquished ferocity, similar to how the romantics had viewed them a half century earlier. A 1916 article in *National Geographic* by a travel writer, Gilbert H. Grosvenor, called "The Land of the Best," described the Indians as "Redskins upon our own Western [*sic*] plains and in *our own* cliff dwellings [who] reveal stories of the past as strange as any we know, and constitute a race more magnificent in physique than any that can be found in other parts of the world" (my italics).[31] A similar 1910 travel article described an evening a tourist might spend "at home" with "bright and cheerful Zuni men and women" and noted the "picturesque" nature of Hopi ceremonies, as if these friendly, "good" Indians were eager to please tourists and invite strangers into their homes.[32] Railroad promotions, such as a 1930 Union Pacific brochure advertising passenger trains through Arizona that featured Maynard Dixon's romanticized painting of an Apache man, depicted Indians as a quaint "lost race," the scattered remains of which were now available for viewing by rail tourists and, by this time, by auto tourists on Route 66 as well.[33] The intrusion of industrial commerce, both rail and road, into the Southwest offered a point of contrast with the artifacts of aboriginal cultures. The decayed state of local ruins reinforced the assumption of many Anglo visitors that modern solutions were more effective than traditional lifestyles.[34] What conclusions twenty-first-century tourists reach when they witness the crumbling ruins of Route 66 will be discussed later.

With the region safe for vacationers, the AT&SF Railroad stepped up its efforts, first promoting the Southwest's scenery and then its native cultures. They sought to advance the notion that a safe but interesting version of the American frontier environment could now be experienced.[35] In 1892 the railroad commissioned the renowned painter, Thomas Moran, to paint landscapes of the Grand Canyon. Seeing the success of earlier efforts, the AT&SF's managers decided to intensify their efforts to encourage tourism and set about hiring artists, photographers, and ethnographers to depict Indian life and natural scenery in the region and planning the construction of large hotels.[36] In 1898, the Southern Pacific Railroad began publishing a promotional tourism periodical, *Sunset*, to increase tourist ridership along its lines.[37] William H. Simpson, who headed the AT&SF's advertising department from 1900 to 1933, assembled a collection of over six hundred paintings, mostly of Pueblo and Navajo scenes, and used them to illustrate colorful AT&SF calendars, which reached as many as three hundred thousand offices, houses, and schools a year.[38]

After 1905, Indians and Indian art and architecture appeared in nearly all AT&SF and Southern Pacific advertisements. A December 1910 layout artfully depicts a romanticized encounter between an Anglo woman tourist and an aloof Native American woman who is selling artifacts. A similar 1912 promotion shows three Indians wrapped in blankets standing in front of a pueblo seen through a contemplative female tourist's train window.[39] Both ads emphasize the contrast between the tourist, who the viewer is probably supposed to identify with, and the exotic otherness of the Native American (figure 1).

In addition to objectifying the Indians themselves, railroad publications also exploited Indian ruins, particularly the ancient Anasazi pueblos. The advertisements featured pictures of natural wonders such as the Painted Desert and Petrified Forest, AT&SF trains puffing through the desert, Indian-made artifacts, and even recently built picturesque Harvey hotels. The stylized, dignified, but perhaps primitive image of a southwestern Indian became the symbol of the AT&SF and the company gave its trains such names as "The Navajo," "The Chief," and "The Super Chief."[40] AT&SF brochures even spoke of the "Santa Fe Indian" and the "Santa Fe Southwest."[41]

The Fred Harvey Company sought to create an aura, a sense of authenticity, for the images they marketed. For example, at its Mexican and Indian House in Albuquerque, the company's designers choreographed the tourist experience to create demand for their merchandise and increase sales, much as many museums do today. First, guides took tourists through an artfully displayed collection of genuine antique Native American and Hispanic artifacts to inspire a sense of wonder and then led them straight into the gift shop where they could purchase handmade reproductions.[42]

Marketing by the railroads and roadside trading posts degraded southwestern art, pottery, and jewelry. Traders encouraged Indian artisans to redesign their wares to suit Anglo tastes rather than create them for tribal use as they had for thousands of years. Traditional silver and turquoise jewelry became lighter, and more ornate and traditional pottery was reduced in size as artisans ceased making functional vessels, such as large water jars, and crafted ornamental pottery instead.[43] Imported materials sometimes replaced traditional ones. Art dealer Frederick Douglas wrote in 1931: "Pieces of old rubber phonograph records are replacing old black jet or lignite. Coral imported from Italy has supplanted almost altogether the reddish-pink stone seen in prehistoric inlay. Within the last five years large quantities of Chinese turquoise have been imported and sold to the Indians."[44] Tailoring crafts for tourist consumption provided needed income for tribes but altered their way of life irreversibly.

By the dawn of the Route 66 era, Indian art had been transformed by the American economy. The Pueblo Indians had been drawn into the national and international art markets. Their artifacts (such as

FIGURE 1. The strange world outside this
tourist's window included Pueblo architecture.
Santa Fe advertisement in *Harper's Magazine*, 1912.

jewelry and pottery) and even their traditional cultural ceremonies
(such as the Snake Dance) had become commodities for the tourist,
with the Fred Harvey Company and roadside trading posts acting as
retailers. Heritage tourism—the conversion of traditional Indian culture and scenery into profits for local businessmen and America's first
giant corporations, the railroads—had come to the Southwest.

Ever-increasing tourism encouraged the railroads to build more rail lines, better roads to get tourists to sites, and additional hotels and restaurants. By the 1920s, the railroad had become so integrated into the New Mexico and Arizona landscape that some tourists asked their guides why the Indians had built their pueblos so far from the tracks.[45] In 1926, to compete with increasing use of the automobile, the Fred Harvey Company launched a tour service called the Harveycar "Indian Detours" to provide chauffeured auto trips from train stations to out-of-the-way scenic areas and Indian sites. The Indian Detours not only gave rail tourists access to areas remote from the tracks but also provided them with appealing, young female guides called Harvey girls. A 1929 Harveycar promotion states, "Those who are passing on into the setting sun made the Southwest safe. The railroad made its gateways accessible. It needed only the automobile, dragging better roads behind it, to let down the last barriers of time and distance, discomfort and inconvenience, that for so long barred the Southwest to any but the pioneer."[46] When Harvey promoters wrote this passage they did not realize that the automobiles they were praising spelled the doom of the very railroad tourism that had made Fred Harvey successful. Competition from the "automobile, dragging better roads behind it," would soon eclipse rail travel. Route 66 was just over two years old.

In addition to helping create the western Indian stereotype that would later appear on Route 66, the AT&SF helped establish the architectural precedents for Route 66's pueblo- and Spanish colonial–revival style motels and cafes. Around the turn of the twentieth century, the AT&SF built and operated an extensive system of hotels throughout the Southwest, which the railroad contracted the Fred Harvey Company to manage. While touring the massive 1893 Colombian Exposition in Chicago, AT&SF executives became inspired by the California Building's mission-style architecture and began using that style in new depots from Kansas to California. The Southern Pacific and Union Pacific soon followed the Santa Fe's lead.[47] AT&SF regionally themed hotels included the Casteñeda in Las Vegas, New Mexico, built in 1899, the Alvarado in Albuquerque built in 1902, and the El Tovar beside the Grand Canyon, built in 1905.[48] The AT&SF encouraged Hopi and Navajo to sell jewelry to tourists at El Tovar. The railroad also built a museum next door in the pueblo-revival style, called the "Hopi House," to display local Native

American artifacts to visitors. The hotel paid Hopi dancers to perform for their guests in the evening.[49]

Architect Mary Jane Colter designed many AT&SF hotels. She began working for the Fred Harvey Company in 1902, having been hired to design the interior of the Alvarado Indian-Mexican building in Albuquerque. Her architecture and interiors borrowed forms from Native American and Mexican-Spanish examples found throughout the Southwest, such as Anasazi watchtowers and Navajo pueblos, and created a "fiction in three dimensions" by exaggerating and condensing regional motifs with the purpose of effecting an artificial aura of regional character and authenticity for tourists.[50]

Colter antiqued many of her buildings to give them a false patina. For example, she blackened fireplace stones to make them look long-used and incorporated genuine Anasazi petroglyphs into stone surfaces, even designing false doorways filled with loose stones to appear, as she wrote, "as if done in haste in the fear of the attack of an enemy."[51] In her more than forty years working for the Fred Harvey Company, Colter designed popular and much-visited structures including the El Navajo in Gallup, New Mexico, built in 1918 and expanded in 1923, and the previously mentioned Hopi House at the Grand Canyon (1905) made to look like "an authentic pueblo dwelling." Five of her buildings, including the Indian Watchtower, are currently National Historic Landmarks.[52]

One significant pueblo-revival hotel located on Route 66 during the eleven years from 1927 to 1938 that the highway passed through Santa Fe was the La Fonda Hotel in downtown Santa Fe, built in 1920. The Santa Fe Railroad bought the hotel in 1925 and leased it to the Fred Harvey Company, which extensively remodeled the building with the help of Mary Jane Colter to make it resemble the Taos and Acoma pueblos. This "inn at the end of the trail" became a significant Route 66 landmark and acted as a venue in which to merchandise Indian crafts, sell regional food, and showcase local residents to early Route 66 travelers.[53]

Another precedent for the many pueblo-style motels on Route 66, especially in New Mexico, originated with the Museum of New Mexico's board of directors including Edgar Lee Hewitt and Charles Lummis, a Harvard-educated journalist and booster of the Southwest credited with coining the term "Southwest" and the phrase "see America first."[54] The directors sought to preserve the historic buildings of Santa Fe and pushed for a new style (the pueblo revival) based on the region's vernacular (Indian and Spanish) traditions. Members of the museum's board exerted great influence on Santa Fe's city government and, after 1912, the city standardized its architecture in the pueblo-revival style, primarily to encourage tourism.

Although based on pueblo and Spanish-mission motifs, new buildings such as the New Mexico State Museum on the plaza in Santa Fe "corrected" the old forms by spacing beams evenly and centering doorways. The new buildings caused confusion because tourists arriving either by rail or on Route 66 often mistook these reproductions for original Indian and Spanish colonial designs. Anglo developers also remodeled actual historic buildings such as the Palace of the Governors on the Santa Fe Plaza to conform to their rationalized version of what they thought pueblo and Spanish architecture should have been.[55]

In addition to marketing Native American cultures, the railroads and their allies marketed Spanish-colonial and Mexican-American cultures. In the nineteenth and early twentieth centuries, the Anglo view of Hispanics was ambivalent and dualistic. On one hand, they viewed Mexican-Americans, or "Spaniards" as they were sometimes called, as colorful and festive dons and beautiful señoritas who took life at a refreshingly slow pace.[56] On the other, Anglos sometimes portrayed Mexicans as wasting time and resources. In *Two Years Before the Mast*, a popular book about his travels published in 1840, Richard Henry Dana Jr. characterized Californios as inhabiting a country (California) that could have been developed and "properly utilized" by a more "industrious race," such as the Anglo-Saxons. "In the hands of an enterprising people," he concludes, "what a country this might be."[57]

Charles F. Lummis wrote *The Land of Poco Tiempo* (the land of "slow time") in 1893, at the time when the AT&SF was just starting to use regional cultures and history in its advertisements. In that book, he described Hispanic New Mexico as "the land of *Poco Tiempo*—the home of pretty soon. . . . The pretty soon of New Spain is better than the Now! Now! of the haggard states. The opiate sun soothes to rest, the adobe is made to lean against, the hush of daylong noon would not be broken. Let us not hasten, *mañana* will do."[58] This passage, which reads like promotional travel literature, perhaps helped invent the clichéd image of the "lazy" Mexican American slumped against an adobe wall, one that appeared at sites on Route 66 such as the La Cita Mexican Foods Restaurant in Tucumcari (figure 2). Lummis reveals his racist view of native New Mexicans later in his book when he describes them as the "in-bred and isolation-shrunken descendants of the Castilian world."[59]

The Fred Harvey Company consistently paid less attention to Mexican Americans than to Native Americans. One of the company's promotional souvenir books, *The Camera of the Southwest*, included pictures of bullfights, burros, and begging Hispanics, but dismissed Spanish influence by stating that it "never took hearty root in this land," and that the influence had "failed." Despite this, the Santa Fe used the allure of the "romance of the old Spanish days" in an ad for the California Limited in 1909. References to Mexicans in company publications and postcards diminished over time.[60] Although the railroads did not glorify Mexican Americans as much as Pueblo Indians, tired burros pulling dilapidated wooden carts, Mexican workers on perpetual siesta, heroic matadors in garish outfits, and fiery señoritas looking more Hollywood than Tijuana made their way to postcards and advertisements throughout the railroad and the Route 66 eras.

A major tribute to the Southwest's Spanish heritage was to give hotels, motels, and other tourist-related businesses Spanish names, such as Fred Harvey's El Tovar Hotel, Hotel El Rancho on Route 66 in Gallup, New Mexico, and the La Siesta Motel in Winslow, Arizona, also on Route 66. These names sought to confirm the public concept of the Wild West, derived from western novels and western movies where Hispanics and Hispanic culture often provided a backdrop for the adventures of Anglo cowboy heroes.

Like Pueblo Indians and Mexican Americans, cowboys became a lasting symbol of the "Old West" on Route 66. During the heyday of actual cowboys, between about 1865 and 1890, the public generally viewed them with suspicion. Cowpunchers, as they were sometimes called, enjoyed little status in the public eye because they were essentially itinerant, unskilled workers who had to endure months of physical strain and boredom and who tended to become drunk and rowdy when they came into town.[61] The cowboy first became a marketable commodity in 1884 when William F. Cody introduced William Levi Taylor, a Texas cowpuncher, to the audiences of his Buffalo Bill's Wild West Show as "Buck Taylor, King of the Cowboys." Cody carefully molded Taylor into an entertainer who portrayed himself as a "wistful

FIGURE 2. La Cita Mexican restaurant on Route 66
in Tucumcari, New Mexico. Photo by author, August 2003.

soul who seemed to be longing for a return to the bucolic environs of
the Great Plains." In 1887, with the publication of *Buck Taylor: King
of the Cowboys; or, The Raiders and the Rangers: A Story of the Wild
and Thrilling Life of William L. Taylor,* Taylor became the first cowboy
hero in fiction.[62]

Although eastern newspapers had eagerly covered events such

as the "true adventures of Billy the Kid" and the shootout at the O.K. Corral, it was pulp fiction that made the cowboy famous.[63] The life and image of the cowboy became legend in books such as Owen Wister's *The Virginian* (1902) and Zane Grey's *The Heritage of the Desert* (1910). Western fiction writers quickly abandoned dull but truthful accounts of cowboy life such as Andy Adam's *The Log of a Cowboy* (1903) and began to build a mythic, heroic figure.

Once the West had been "civilized" by Fred Harvey and after the U.S. Census Bureau announced that the western frontier no longer existed in 1890, the cowboy became a symbol of a lost "golden era" of "frontier culture" where honor, justified violence, freedom, and primitive democracy ruled.[64] Theodore Roosevelt espoused this concept of the "democratic life of the cowboy" in his 1913 *Autobiography*. Roosevelt saw cowboys as independent Anglo-Saxons uncontaminated by urban maladies, such as "the poison of labor unionism." Roosevelt described cowpunchers as "hardy and self-reliant as any man who ever breathed—with bronzed, set faces and keen eyes that look all the world in the face without flinching as they flash out from under the broad-rimmed hats."[65] Roosevelt idealized cowboys as embodying the masculine "strenuous life," which he prescribed as a cure for the ills of an increasingly industrial and sedentary society.[66]

Although Owen Wister made a series of visits to the West, he wrote *The Virginian* as "a Pennsylvanian who sat in South Carolina to write a book about a Virginian living in Wyoming."[67] The fact that a Philadelphia blue blood wrote *The Virginian* did not prevent this pioneering work of the western fiction genre from selling over one hundred thousand copies in its first year. Wister's book was made into a silent movie in 1914 and a talkie in 1929 starring Gary Cooper.[68] The story pitted cowboys against rustlers and invented the Main Street shoot-out so often found in westerns. Wister didn't depict cowboys engaging in the dull practice of herding cattle in *The Virginian* but, like Zane Grey, blurred the distinction between cowboys and gun fighters and helped create the image of the heroic individualist hero in a ten-gallon hat wearing a six-gun and a bandana, riding a horse with ropes over his saddle.

Like Roosevelt, Wister was xenophobic. He and many of his successors saw the cowboy as the last cavalier. In 1895 he wrote, "to survive in clean cattle country requires spirit of adventure, courage, and self-sufficiency; you will not find many Poles or Huns or Russian

Jews in that district. The Anglo-Saxon is still forever homesick for the out-of-doors."[69] Wister regarded the cowboy as an incarnation of a mythic, rugged Anglo-Saxon racial heritage akin to the "knight in shining armor."

Wister's notion of cowboy demographics was not accurate. In the early 1880s, at the height of the great cattle drives, one in three western cowboys was black or Mexican.[70] Still, the image of the Anglo cowboy hero flourished. The 25 percent of cowboys who were black and 12 percent who were Mexican did not suit the racial mores of the times,[71] so fiction writers and their audiences played up the pale version of the cowboy instead.

Zane Grey, like Wister, played a pivotal role in permanently fixing western myths and imagery in the minds of the public. In the course of his writing career, which lasted from 1910 to 1932, he wrote fifty-five novels and by 1936 he had sold over twelve million books. Read by millions of Americans, Grey's books made *Bookman's* top ten best-seller list every year between 1917 and 1924. By 1956 Grey had sold 68 million books worldwide and by 1984 130 million had been printed. The over one hundred western movies based on his novels multiplied the impact of his work. Virtually all tourists old or young who traveled Route 66 had read a western book or had seen a western movie and most had probably read and seen many.

Actual cowboy celebrities were not always Anglo-Saxon. Will Rogers, who gave Route 66 one of its many nicknames, was proudly part Cherokee. Born in 1879 near Claremore, Oklahoma (which would become a Route 66 community in 1927), Rogers projected the heroic cowboy image, wearing a "ten-gallon hat, a snug flaming red flannel shirt, fancy vest, knotted red bandanna and trousers tucked into high-heeled, gleaming boots with jingling spurs."[72] In the 1910s, he starred in fifty silent movies and became a world-famous radio and newspaper commentator in the 1920s. Rogers traveled the world, making the cowboy and his home state of Oklahoma famous.[73] After his tragic death in an air crash in 1935, Route 66 became known as the Will Rogers Highway. The Will Rogers Motor Court, located in Tulsa, which had a cowboy and a lasso incorporated into its sign was a Route 66 mainstay, and the Will Rogers Hotel in Claremore still casts its shadow on the highway. Tourist postcards often called Oklahoma "Will Rogers Country," helping to associate Route 66 with the myth of the heroic cowboy.

The idea of Indians, Mexicans, and cowboys, developed in railroad brochures, western novels, and western movies, formed the foundation for much of the imagery found on Route 66. It seems fitting that Route 66 became the primary autoroute to Hollywood, the center of filmmaking. Southern California became a node of "cowboy culture" because of the vast popularity of the western genre of motion picture. After 1909, the annual routine of many actual cowboys involved three seasons: the spring rodeo circuit, the fall cattle roundup, and a winter stop in southern California where they would congregate in Hollywood bars hoping to be selected by film production crews as stunt men and extras.[74] This nexus among real cowboys such as Will Rogers, faux Indians, and stereotyped Mexicans with the California film industry helped cement the western myth on which Route 66 thrived.

As the popularity of the Southwest grew, the nature of transportation in the United States changed. By the late 1920s, automobiles had come into intense competition with the railroads. Although passenger lines held a substantial portion of market until after the Second World War, they slowly started losing customers to autos after 1915.

Gradual and seamless, the transition from trains to automobiles helped open the region to vast numbers of tourists who would remember traveling on Route 66 as an integral part of their southwestern experience.

After 1926, many early railroad communities became Route 66 towns, and roadside business and local chambers of commerce adopted the icons that the railroads used to promote tourism on Route 66. The myth of the Southwest became so powerful in the twentieth century that it helped transform the region as newcomers and businesses altered the landscape through architecture, especially the pueblo- and Spanish-colonial revival, to satisfy tourist expectations (plates 4A and B). Harvey Houses and Santa Fe stations had a direct impact on Route 66 travelers and merchants because the AT&SF lines paralleled and often crossed the Route 66 corridor. One railroad-era hotel, Fred Harvey's El Navajo Hotel in Gallup, New Mexico, was in plain view of Highway 66 (plate 3). In fact it was so close to Route 66 that most of it had to be demolished to make way for a widening of the highway in 1957.[75]

The tourist court and motel industry in the Southwest and elsewhere quickly copied the pueblo revival and mission revival from the railroads and from the cities of Santa Fe and to a lesser degree, Albuquerque. With the advent of mass auto tourism, the pueblo- and Spanish–colonial revival styles passed from the realm of the high style, academic architecture of Mary Colter and Charles Lummis into the popular, commercial buildings of the roadside.[76] From the 1920s to the 1970s, motel developers built pueblo-style buildings up and down Route 66 and on other highways in places as disparate as Florida, Nevada, and Missouri. Several noteworthy examples built on Route 66 are the El Vado Motel in Albuquerque, New Mexico, the Zuni Court, also in Albuquerque, and the Park Plaza Motel chain in St. Louis, Tulsa, Amarillo, and Flagstaff.[77] In addition, builders constructed "wigwam" tourist courts with teepee-shaped cabins in Arizona and California on Route 66 to exploit the region's association with Indians.

The transition from train to auto tourism created new challenges for the marketing of the Southwest. A wide range of small, private, vernacular marketing efforts replaced the controlled, centralized, corporate railroad publicity programs. Roadside businesses created a roadside marketplace using much of the same imagery as the railroads, but in more eccentric, abstract, and diverse forms.

CHAPTER TWO

The Rise of a Celebrity

A Short History of Route 66

Between 1900 and 1940, automobiles gradually overtook the passenger railroads and came to dominate transportation and tourism in the United States. The number of automobiles rose dramatically. In 1905 Americans had registered only approximately 78,000 vehicles, but by 1910 that number climbed to 458,500. In 1921 alone, Americans purchased over 1.6 million cars, and by the late 1920s Americans had registered a total of over 23 million.[1]

Owing to automobiles, in the 1920s a much greater number of Americans were able to take vacations than had been able to during the railroad era. The Middletown study of 1929 reported that: "Use of the automobile has . . . been influential in spreading the 'vacation' habit . . . 'Vacations in 1890?' echoed one substantial citizen, 'why the word wasn't in the dictionary!'"[2]

At first, however, motorcars were luxuries that only the affluent could afford. But using modern industrial methods, producers such as Henry Ford responded quickly to increasing public demand and soon supplied the American people with large numbers of comparatively inexpensive vehicles. In 1912, Ford Motor Company introduced the assembly-line-produced Model T, a car that Ford advertised as built for "every man." The Model T cost only $650, about the price of a small economy car today (approximately $13,300 in 2006 dollars).[3] Other companies soon followed Ford's lead, and ownership of automobiles quickly expanded among middle-class Americans.[4]

At first, automobiles had little practical application for long-distance trips because a viable road system had not yet been constructed, but a small number of Americans did take to the crude, dirt roads in their new cars to explore the vast continent. Automobile producers even hired professional drivers to take long trips in their cars to publicize the possibility of using their vehicles for tourism. In 1902 the Packard Motor Car Company sent Tom Fetch, a mechanic, writer, and photographer and several others on a fifty-one-day journey from San Francisco to New York in a Packard dubbed "Old Pacific." Fetch and his companions took a large number of photos to document their trip across the rural landscape. Six years later in 1908, crossing the continent in sixty to ninety days in a car was considered "good time for a non-professional driver."[5] Despite the difficulties, enthusiasm for auto vacations grew rapidly.

Automobile tourism began as a spontaneous activity called auto camping or "gypsying," when a small but growing number of upper-middle-class Americans chose to spend their vacations driving across vast expanses of the country, particularly the West and South.[6] Auto camping appealed to affluent but unconventional families who wanted to explore the countryside without having to endure the old-fashioned formalities and strict etiquette required by railroads, railroad hotels, and ships.

Early auto travel was arduous and closer to nature than train travel and revived the leisurely pace, freedom of movement, simplicity, and family solidarity of bygone times when families drove horse- or ox-drawn wagons but with increased range and speed.[7] Expressing the American tradition of rugged individualism, auto gypsies helped define the concept of the "freedom of the open road," which Walt Whitman described in his 1855 poem "Song of the Open Road."[8] With roots in Whitman and the auto gypsies, references to the open road abound in Route 66 literature.

The rapid increase in automobile use in the early twentieth century led to demand for smoother and more direct roads, and in 1912 a diverse group of activist citizens and businesspeople began a grass-roots crusade for long-distance highways. This coalition of road boosters, which included car owners, automakers, petroleum companies, brick and asphalt producers, and owners of restaurants and other roadside businesses, became the "good roads movement."[9]

Good roads associations usually formed to promote a specific route. The first such organization, the Lincoln Highway Association, was established in 1912 when Carl Graham Fisher, a well-known promoter of Florida real estate and founder of the Indianapolis Motor Speedway, proposed creating the first coast-to-coast highway.[10] At this time, the United States had no long-distance paved roads and had no coast-to-coast motor routes of any kind. Existing roads twisted across the countryside, often leading drivers in indirect routes or even in circles, much as small country roads do today.[11] Nearly all roads in North America had a dirt surface, which became dusty and ribbed in dry weather, muddy and nearly impassable in wet weather, and were almost always pocked with large bumps and potholes that slowed travel to a crawl. Even roads within villages and cities usually remained unpaved, and the best, so-called improved roads generally had nothing more than a gravel surface.

The Lincoln Highway Association became the first of a number of highway organizations formed to promote and construct specific, named highways: the Dixie Highway Association, founded in 1915 to promote a highway from Chicago, Illinois, to Miami, Florida;[12] the Lee Highway Association formed in 1919 to promote a route from Canada to New Orleans that later became U.S. Highway 11; and the Old Spanish Trail Association, formed in 1915 to create a highway along the Gulf Coast that essentially became U.S. Route 90 in 1927.[13] Although private contributions funded early construction of long-distance roads, state and federal funds would be required to build highways on a large scale. In 1912, only twenty-eight of the forty-eight states had spent any money at all on roads, but this would soon change. By 1922 the United States had spent over two billion dollars on roads.[14]

As with the Lincoln Highway and other named highways, a good roads association helped to create the named predecessors of Route 66. Shortly after the establishment of the Lincoln Highway Association in 1912, good roads boosters conceived a "National Old Trails Road" that would link Washington, D.C., to San Diego, California. Shortly thereafter, the National Old Trails Road Association formed to promote a coast-to-coast highway concept that followed existing railroad alignments and roughly paralleled a series of old wagon roads, including Beale's Road. The "National Old Trails Road" followed the old Cumberland Road from Washington, D.C., to St. Louis and from there traced the old Santa Fe Trail southwest to Albuquerque, then up to Santa Fe and then followed the approximate path of the Santa Fe Railroad tracks across western New Mexico, Arizona, and down into southern California. Another named highway that traced a portion of future Route 66 was the Panhandle Pacific Highway, which crossed the panhandle of Texas into New Mexico, passing through Tucumcari, Santa Rosa, and Vaughn. Yet another ancestor of Route 66 in New Mexico was the western branch of the Ozark Trails Highway, known in the early 1920s as the Old Postal Highway.[15]

Farther north, the first motorway between St. Louis and Chicago was the Pontiac Trail, established in 1915. The state of Illinois later designated this road Illinois Route 4 and financed the construction of eighteen-foot-wide paved segments that Route 66 would soon incorporate. Using horse teams and surplus World War I trucks, contractors often excavated fill from nearby borrow pits, many of which became the fishponds that can still be seen along historic Route 66.[16] Although the Illinois section of future Route 66 (Illinois Route 4) between Chicago and St. Louis was nearly paved by 1924, the sections of future Route 66 to the West, such as the Old Trails Highway, remained a series of dirt tracks.

Soon after the good roads movement formed, the federal government began funding road construction in response to the explosion in automobile production and political pressure from the highway associations, which often had influential members. In 1916, the United States Congress passed the Federal Aid Road Act (the Shackleford Bill), which appropriated seventy-five million dollars for road building to be distributed to the states over five years. Congress allocated the money for the construction of dirt and gravel rural roads in less affluent states and for paved highways in urban areas.[17] This legislation made the federal government the primary financer of long-distance highways, a role that it has played ever since.[18]

With federal money and an onslaught of automobiles, road builders worked quickly to transform the railroad-oriented landscape along the Route 66 corridor into an automobile-oriented one. When engineers laid out the predecessors of Route 66, such as Illinois Route 4, they built the highway parallel to the tracks and sometimes traced old wagon roads that the tracks had followed when they were constructed.

Building alongside the tracks allowed road contractors to utilize the gentle grades and smooth curves that railroad designers fashioned to make the tracks usable by trains. According to Rufous Carter, who worked as a design engineer for the New Mexico Highway Department in the 1920s, following railroad rights-of-way allowed road engineers to use "the other guy's knowledge."[19]

In most towns, Route 66 passed late-nineteenth- and early-twentieth-century commercial buildings that were built facing the tracks and that, in an effort to advertise the town's existence to passing railroad passengers were designed with false fronts to make them look large and fancy. Building facades and accompanying signage showed tourists that the community offered services to passengers who changed trains or elected to stop and spend the night.[20] When auto tourists began coming through these same communities, businesses simply added motorists as clients.

As the number of motorists increased and the number of railroad passengers declined along the corridor, the commercial orientation of new businesses shifted from the tracks to the highway. However, most railroad-era buildings remained, and established enterprises such as hotels, restaurants, and shops continued operating alongside newer, road-related diners and tourist courts, especially in the early years. Many proprietors of businesses that had previously served wagons and stagecoaches, such as livery stables and trading posts, converted their establishments into filling stations and roadside attractions.

The Domingo Trading Post in New Mexico successfully made the transition from serving railroad passengers to motorists. This business served local customers and railroad travelers who stopped to visit the nearby Santo Domingo Pueblo, and when automobiles arrived, the curio shop began serving auto tourists with the same enthusiasm as it had railroad customers.[21]

The transition from railroad to highway business did cause some conflict. A number of merchants feared that the development of a long-distance highway would benefit only garages, motels, and gas stations located directly on the roadside and that the concentration of business along the highway might decrease significantly the business of downtown retailers and hotels. Members of some rural communities worried that their local economy would become too dependent on the road. An editorial in the December 30, 1926, *Tucumcari News* (New Mexico) stated, "cross-state highways are good for the garages and for hotels," but they "would weaken other Tucumcari businesses."[22] The shift from town centers to the highway was a national phenomenon. One Georgia merchant commented in 1926, "The place of trade is where the automobiles go. . . . A central location is no longer a good one."[23]

Regardless of the disruptions to businesses they caused, long-distance highways were the wave of the future. Funding for highways became an annual federal appropriation beginning in 1926. Late in that same year, the federal government replaced the confusing web of over 250 individually and privately marked and named highways that had sprung up since 1912 with a rational system of numbered routes.[24]

One of the most influential promoters of the Federal Highway Act of 1921 and the numbering of federal highways in late 1926 was Cyrus Avery, whose primary motivation was that he wanted a major interstate route through his home state of Oklahoma. In 1921, members of the Associated Highways Association, an umbrella group for forty-two individual good roads organizations such as the Dixie Highway and Old Trails Highway Associations, elected Avery as its president. Avery also led the American Association of State Highway Officials, which called for a "comprehensive system of through interstate routes and a uniform scheme for designating such routes." Responding to pressure from the American Association of State Highway Officials, the United States Congress passed a comprehensive highway bill in 1925 and directed the secretary of agriculture to appoint a twenty-one member committee to negotiate with state highway departments to "devise a uniform scheme" of highways.[25]

This committee decided to assign numbers to 96,626 miles of major highways to avoid the confusion created by the large number of intertwined, named roads. The group systematically assigned the primary north-south "trunk" routes with numbers ending in "1" or "5" and gave the primary east-west roads numbers ending in "0." The committee assigned northern highways low numbers, such as Route 10 and gave each major road to the south a successively higher number. The most southerly trunk route, Route 90, crossed Florida and continued west through the Deep South along the Gulf Coast and then traversed central Texas before terminating just above the Mexican border in El Paso.[26] The committee also adopted new black-and-white shield-shaped signs to mark the recently designated federal highways. Avery, who acted as a consulting highway specialist to this group, used his influence to advocate routing a major east-west highway through his home city of Tulsa, Oklahoma, and west through Oklahoma City.[27]

Ironically, the famous number "66" was Avery's second choice. Avery and his allies asked the federal committee to designate their Chicago to Los Angeles route Route 60, but the governor of Kentucky, W. J. Fields, and highway officials from Virginia objected because they were planning their own Route 60 from Newport News to Springfield, Missouri.[28] Avery's road planners even printed thousands of maps showing a "Route 60" passing through Oklahoma. However, the Upper-South group would not relent and finally forced Avery's faction to pick "66" as their highway's official number. On November 11, 1926, Congress approved the new highway numbering system, which included "Route 66" from Chicago to Los Angeles.[29]

When highway enthusiasts received the new maps, they noticed the great, diagonal arc that Route 66 made across the western half of North America and decided to use the highway's unusual alignment and its catchy number as marketing tools. They would often feature colorful maps boldly marked "Route 66" on postcards and brochures.[30]

After its official designation, Route 66 went through five distinct periods in which its general character and dominant uses changed. From 1927 to about 1934, the road functioned as a newly opened tour route and early trunk highway, and remained in a rugged state in most areas, especially in the West. Between 1934 and 1940, Route 66 became the "road of flight" for hundreds of thousands of economic refugees from Oklahoma and surrounding states fleeing the Dust Bowl. Army convoys frequented the road from 1940 to 1945, and the highway was also the site of POW camps and mock battles. After 1945, Route 66 became a heavily traveled tour route and the primary transportation corridor between Chicago and Los Angeles. Finally, from 1956 through the late 1970s, segments of new, divided, limited access interstate highways gradually replaced Route 66, now a highway in decline. Segments of the old road remained in service as part of the primary route until 1984, when Interstate Highway 40 bypassed the last section of Route 66 through Williams, Arizona.[31] The federal government officially decommissioned Route 66 in 1985.

At the beginning of the first era, which lasted from 1927 to 1934, Cyrus Avery and John T. Woodruff met with delegates from five of the highway's eight states and formed the U.S. 66 Highway Association to promote the newly created route. The association worked to increase tourism by actively publicizing the highway, which they dubbed the "Main Street of America." The organization issued guidebooks, maps, and postcards to entice tourists to travel west or east on Route 66 instead of taking alternate roads such as U.S. 30 and U.S. 40. In cooperation with Route 66 businesses, the association organized and promoted "Indian Shows," athletic events, rodeos, regional fairs, and tours to keep Route 66 in the minds of as many people as possible.[32] In 1927 association leaders traveled along the highway in a Pickwick bus "fitted up like a Pullman Sleeper" and met with local community boosters in Springfield, Missouri; Amarillo, Texas; and Albuquerque, New Mexico, to coordinate promotional efforts.[33]

Perhaps the most sensational of the Route 66 Association's early publicity efforts was the Great Transcontinental Footrace. C. C. Pyle, known as the P. T. Barnum of professional sports, promoted a pedestrian race from Los Angeles to New York. The racecourse covered the entire 2,448-mile length of Route 66 and then continued east from Chicago to New York. Pyle's so-called bunion derby got underway in the spring of 1928, when 275 runners paid a $100 (about $1,192 in 2006 dollars) entrance fee and set out from Los Angeles for New York, hoping to collect the $25,000 (about $294,000 in 2006 dollars)[34] grand prize and smaller prizes for second through tenth place. Amazingly, fifty runners managed to cross the finish line in New York in eighty-seven days or more after they began in Los Angeles. Andy Payne, a farm boy from Oklahoma who was part Cherokee, won the race, finishing ahead of many seasoned marathoners. He used a portion of the money to pay off his parent's mortgage. Although C. C., now known as "Corn and Callus" Pyle, lost over sixty thousand dollars on the project, the footrace became a significant event on Route 66's path to fame.[35]

After the race, the Route 66 Association continued to promote the highway as a tourist route. The association placed its first advertisement in a national magazine. The ad, which appeared in the July 16, 1932, issue of the *Saturday Evening Post* and covered a full column, invited Americans to travel the "Great Diagonal Highway" to the 1932 Olympic Games in Los Angeles. Within a week, the U.S. 66 Highway Association office in Tulsa, Oklahoma, received hundreds of requests for information.[36]

The U.S. 66 Highway Association was not the only entity to promote southwestern attractions in the late 1920s and early 1930s. The railroads, which had marketed southwestern attractions and Indian art for several decades, continued these publicity campaigns into the 1950s. Western Route 66 chambers of commerce and roadside merchants also recruited tourists to the region by marketing local cultures, Hollywood myths about the West, and natural beauty as attractions.

Events in the 1920s helped popularize southwestern Indian art. In 1922 the Gallup, New Mexico, Chamber of Commerce, seeking to draw tourists to the region, organized the first Intertribal Indian Ceremonial. The ceremonial, which became an annual event, involved days of exhibitions, cultural displays, and craft shows by tribes. The show emphasized quality Native American crafts over dancing.

In 1925, the state of New Mexico established an Indian arts fund to create more demand for Indian-made crafts, and in the late 1920s, Indian schools in the Southwest began to encourage their students to learn and produce traditional crafts that they would modify for tourists. Selling to railroad passengers and automobilists on Route 66 provided isolated and cash-poor tribes and local merchants with a needed source of hard currency but, as discussed in chapter 1, creating art for tourists also eroded tribal traditions.[37]

At the time when Native American art was growing in popularity, traffic on Route 66 increased. Much of the initial increase in tourist travel was due to the promotional efforts of booster organizations such as the U.S. 66 Highway Association.[38] In 1925 the New Mexico Office of the State Engineer counted an average of only 207 cars passing each day between Albuquerque and Gallup.[39] Once Route 66 was commissioned in 1926 and promoted, the volume of traffic gradually increased west of St. Louis, even though much of the highway remained unpaved. In 1929 a Texaco road report listed the Illinois segment as completely covered in asphalt or cement. However, the same document reported the road as being only 66 percent paved in Missouri, 25 percent paved in Oklahoma, and completely unpaved from the Texas Panhandle to the outskirts of Los Angeles, California. Traffic along the western segments remained scant until the early 1930s.[40]

Road-related businesses, such as tourist camps, souvenir shops, and cafés that catered to tourists, truckers, business travelers, and people looking for work flourished along the eastern half of Route 66 in the late 1920s. Many small Route 66 towns, such as Chenoa, Illinois, developed intensive service strips, often called "gasoline alleys." In Chenoa, six stations opened along Morehead Street. As in hundreds of similar strips, gas station operators erected large signs and offered amenities such as seating areas, restrooms, "full service" oil checks, and windshield washing to attract customers in an increasingly competitive market.[41] Some gas stations expanded into full-service truck stops with restaurants and gift shops.

The Shirley Oil Company, which opened in 1923 in Shirley, Illinois, moved to Route 66 in McLean in 1928. It changed its name to the Dixie Trucker's Home and became a large, all-night establishment where truckers and motorists could buy fuel, eat, spend the night, and have their cars or trucks serviced. This famous Route 66 business prospered and later expanded into a regional chain.[42]

Clines Corners, a 1934 gas station located on Route 66 in central New Mexico that moved to its present location in 1937, also evolved into an institution along the highway. This business, which started as a small roadside outpost, later grew into a sprawling complex with a vast souvenir shop, an extensive café, and lines of fuel pumps. Clines Corners (plate 5) developed facilities for automobilists, truckers, and recreation vehicle operators. Like the Dixie Trucker's Home, Clines Corners has outlived Route 66 and operates today.[43]

By 1930 the trucking industry began to rival the railroads in the freight business. Truckers favored Route 66 because it provided a road from Chicago to the Pacific that was often more passable in winter than more northern transcontinental highways such as U.S. 30 and U.S. 40.[44] Tourists and increasing numbers of migrants favored automobile travel on Route 66 because the route provided a direct and interesting trip to southern California that offered flexibility and lower costs.

While auto tourism during the latter half of the "Roaring Twenties" laid the foundations for Route 66's rise to fame, the refugees of the Great Depression helped make the highway a cultural icon. In the 1930s, Route 66 became the migratory route for hundreds of thousands of so-called Okies from the southern Great Plains during and after the four years of severe dust storms that became known as the Dust Bowl. Although many Okies actually did use the highway, the plight of the Dust Bowl migrants became directly associated with Route 66 mainly because John Steinbeck emphasized the highway as their "road of flight" to California in *The Grapes of Wrath*, published in 1939.[45]

Between 1931 and 1938 more than 2.5 million people left the Great

Plain states and over 200,000 refugees fled to California, often following Route 66 to a state that only sixty years earlier had available land and offered economic opportunity.[46] By the 1930s, however, California was fully settled, and the migrants found no sanctuary and little opportunity there. In a sense, the American myth that there would always be more land to the west died when the Okies discovered that there was no place for them in California. Many former Okies interviewed by Thomas W. Pew Jr. in 1976 reported that they identified with early pioneers such as "Marcy, Simpson and Beale," who had also "traveled the route and survived."[47] Fewer than 8 percent of the Dust Bowl migrants remained in California more than a few months to a year.[48] For the first time in American history, economic conditions and resistance from residents forced significant numbers of westbound pioneers back east.

Most of the migrants were white. According to a western Oklahoma gas station and motel operator interviewed in 1998, the vast majority on Route 66 who passed her gas station were white people from Arkansas, Oklahoma, and Missouri. When asked why she thought so few African Americans migrated west along Route 66, she said "maybe it was because the blacks were too broke to even leave town."[49] The Great Migration of blacks from the South to the North and West Coast actually slowed during the Depression years and so it makes sense that many African Americans may not have had enough money to travel during the Dust Bowl.[50] Also, the Great Plains, the area hardest hit, did not have a significant black population.

The migrants were victims of dire economic and environmental events. High crop prices during World War I encouraged farmers in the Great Plains to break vast tracts of new lands, but wheat and cotton prices began to decline in the mid-1920s. Cotton prices fell from $22.33 a bale in 1924 to $8.71 a bale in 1930 to a paltry $5.06 a bale in 1931, and prices continued to drop through 1935.[51] Between 1900 and 1929, often using tractors, farmers broke over thirty-two million acres of sod. They plowed in straight rows, which exposed the soil to wind erosion. Until 1931, rain had been sufficient in the West to hold the soils in place, but a severe drought that had started in the East in 1930 moved west that year and caused a chain reaction of dust storms. Great Plains farmers had begun to trickle west in the 1920s, due to crop failures, bank foreclosures, farm consolidations, and the promise of better employment, but the Dust Bowl transformed the trickle into a torrent.[52] Federal New Deal subsidies to landowners who paid for taking land out of production in order to raise crop prices also contributed to tenant farmers being expelled from their land. These programs usually benefited landowners who used the subsidies to consolidate their holdings and buy tractors, reducing the demand for sharecroppers.[53]

John Steinbeck's novel *The Grapes of Wrath*, and John Ford's 1940 movie based on the book, forever linked the plight of the Okies with the "Mother Road," a name that Steinbeck gave to Route 66 when he wrote, "Highway 66 is the main migrant road. 66—the long concrete path across the country, waving gently up and down on the map. . . . 66 is the path of people in flight, refugees from dust and shrinking land, from the thunder of tractors and shrinking ownership. . . . 66 is the mother road, the road of flight."[54]

Images, such as Dorothea Lange's famous portrait of Dust Bowl refugee Florence Thompson's prematurely aged eyes gazing into hopelessness, flanked by the hidden faces of her young children, also helped to memorialize the tragedy. Lange's photographs depicted the Dust Bowl migrants in the arid western landscapes of Route 66 and helped to place their plight in the American consciousness.[55]

A less-documented migration also took place during the Great Depression on Route 66. Many rural families from east of Oklahoma City did not go to California but instead migrated north in search of work. The operator of a roadside restaurant in Illinois on Route 66 in the 1930s described Route 66 during the Depression as "the gateway to the North. During the Depression people went north to Springfield, Detroit, and Chicago looking for work." He described some of these migrants as Mexican Americans traveling to work in the beet fields and cherry orchards of Michigan and other north Midwestern states.[56] In addition, some of the Okies who made a portion of their journey on Route 66 were not from the Great Plains at all but from the Appalachian Mountains of Tennessee, Kentucky, and West Virginia. Nearly a third of the population of these southern states moved into Ohio, Indiana, Michigan, and California during the Depression years.[57]

Displaced tenant farmers comprised only a portion of those who migrated on Route 66 in the 1930s. Some were veterans traveling east, such as a group from the "Bonus Army" of World War I veterans who, in 1932, stayed at a Gallup camp operated by a fellow veteran on their way to Washington, D.C., to protest being denied the bonus promised them by the federal government for fighting in the war.[58] Factory workers and miners, including strikers and strikebreakers, also traveled the road in both directions in search of employment.

Although the U.S. economy remained generally weak during the Great Depression, Route 66 and other long-distance highways acted as an engine of economic activity and growth during these years. A significant reason the highways remained active was that road improvements became a central goal of President Franklin D. Roosevelt's public works programs. For example, the National Industrial Recovery Act of 1933 provided almost six million dollars for road construction in New Mexico alone.[59] Other government efforts to stimulate the economy by providing jobs involved road-building projects, and the entire length of Route 66 was paved by 1937. With failing crops and deflated food prices, road jobs kept many western farmers from becoming migrants in search of work.

Many New Deal road projects addressed safety issues on the highway. As cars were able to go faster and traffic increased, the alignments of the route became dangerous, and accidents increased. Federal money helped to straighten segments of Route 66. Sharp turns were taken out and grade separations were provided at railroad crossings. Many at-grade crossings existed on roads intersecting with Route 66 and across the highway itself because it usually paralleled railroad tracks. These crossings caused many fatal accidents, such as one in 1930 near Isleta Pueblo, New Mexico, where a mail train collided with a Pickwick-Greyhound bus, killing twenty passengers.[60]

During the 1930s, highway builders added new bypasses along the route to bypass narrow, dangerous, and obsolete segments. Highway contractors created new bypasses as better road construction technology and federal funds became available.

Traffic increased on Route 66 throughout the Depression years. The Illinois Division of Highways announced in 1936 that the segment of Route 66 in Illinois represented the most-traveled long-distance highway in the state.[61] In 1931, fifteen hundred trucks passed through St. Louis each day on Route 66. By 1941 that number had increased to seventy-five hundred.[62]

New Deal workers not only built roads but also constructed road-related amenities that enhanced the roadside landscape, such as picnic areas, municipal parks, swimming pools, and bridges. Local residents, migrants, and tourists used these facilities, and many New

Deal-era structures and designed landscapes can still be seen along American highways, including Route 66. New Deal projects such as Five Mile Park west of Tucumcari, New Mexico, and the Santa Rosa city park benefited Route 66 travelers as well as local residents.[63]

Driving west on Route 66 offered a relatively inexpensive vacation during hard times. While thousands of Americans traveled to look for work, others kept their jobs and had enough money to "motor west," sustaining the boom in auto tourism throughout the 1930s. Traffic counts on the Texas-New Mexico border steadily increased throughout the 1930s. Average daily traffic rose from 211 in 1928, to 300 in 1936–37, to 970 in 1941. In addition, the percentage of out-of-state cars increased. Vacationers and migrants had to purchase supplies, and both groups helped support Route 66 businesses.[64]

With the automobile dominant by the late 1930s, the focus shifted away from the deliberate and regulated travel experiences provided by the Fred Harvey Company to the relative chaos of private automobile tourism. In 1937 the American Automobile Association reported that approximately forty-two million Americans toured by car in the previous year and of that number 32.9 percent stopped in tourist courts.[65] Motorists were free to roam when and where they pleased, and they often did just that, driving without a clear itinerary or idea of where they were going. Instead of being directed by railroad guides and "Harvey girls," motorists found themselves being directed by roadside signs promising services ahead and being drawn in by thematic architecture designed to catch their attention and get them to stop. Along the way, they encountered competing tourist attractions and other road-related businesses instead of the choreographed experiences provided by the railroads.

Although the Great Depression hurt the hotel industry and nearly every other type of American business, the burgeoning "tourist cottage," "cabin court," "tourist court," "auto court," "autel," and finally "motel" industry flourished throughout the Depression because people continued to take inexpensive vacations by car and travel the highways to seek employment.[66]

The December 1933 issue of *Architectural Record* estimated that more than four hundred thousand tourist court cabins had been constructed nationally in the Depression years since 1929, representing a total investment of over sixty million dollars.[67] Other road-related businesses also expanded. In the decade after World War I, the nation had experienced a massive increase in the number of roadside restaurants, with the total number jumping over 40 percent between 1910 and 1927. In the early 1920s contractors built gas stations at a rate of more than twelve hundred a year.[68]

In addition to motels and gas stations, many road-related businesses, such as drive-in restaurants, prospered during the Great Depression. An example is the Steak'n Shake Restaurant that opened in 1934 in Normal, Illinois, at a small gas station. Steak'n Shake soon introduced curbside service, allowing Route 66 tourists and locals to eat side-by-side inside their cars. The business, which later became a major restaurant chain, continues to operate today.[69]

During the Depression, some residents of rural communities along Route 66 found that the only way they could remain on their land was to take a risk and invest money, often all they had, to start a road-related business. As contractors constructed new alignments, businesses along the bypassed sections had to relocate. New segments of road offered opportunities for aspiring entrepreneurs to buy land and start service stations, motels, and cafés. Entire towns, such as Moriarty, New Mexico, gravitated toward new segments of highway when they opened. Larger settlements such as Gallup began to develop auto service strips that extended away from town along the highway. Widespread use of the automobile altered the compact configurations of the old railroad towns.[70]

In the late 1930s, tourist courts, diners, and gas stations started becoming more substantial and the signs advertising them more elaborate. Investments in motels in the United States increased throughout the 1930s. A 1939 article in *Tourist Court Journal* estimated that the average investment at the time in a new twenty-unit court was a thousand dollars per unit. The average per-unit investment had been only a hundred dollars in 1925.[71]

Increased investments and competition prompted road-related businesses to erect large neon signs to make their establishments stand out. One distinctive sign on Route 66 was the Navajo Motel sign in Navajo, Arizona, which featured an illustration of James Earle Fraser's *The End of the Trail*, a painting depicting a Native American brave on an exhausted horse.[72] Another is the El Vado Motel sign in Albuquerque, New Mexico, which headlines the image of an Indian "chief" in a headdress. Yet another, the Apache Motel sign in Tucumcari, New Mexico, is shaped like a giant arrowhead (figure 3),

FIGURE 3. Apache Motel, Tucumcari,
New Mexico. Photo by author, March 2006.

and the "Western Motel" sign in Sayre, Oklahoma, features a giant cactus. Many more such signs can still be seen along historic U.S. 66.

In general, motel operators of the 1930s on the eastern half of Route 66 preferred the nostalgic preindustrial image of a formation of rustic cottages in a park-like setting, making a large investment in a glitzy modern establishment unwarranted.[73] Examples include the Ozark Court in Sullivan, Missouri, which had nondescript cabins with gabled roofs and brick exteriors; the Wagon Wheel Motel in Cuba, Missouri, which has stone bungalow-like cabins; and John's Modern Cabins, in Rolla, Missouri, which had log-style cabins. Carpenters and contractors, rather than architects, typically designed and built the cabins. Some mail-order house catalogs, such as the Aladdin catalog from Michigan, sold square, one room, 7' x 12' precut "tourist cottage" kits to motor court operators.[74] Articles in magazines such as *American Builder* advised contractors and owner-builders on how to design and build sturdy, comfortable, and attractive cabins.

On the western half of Route 66, from Texas west, 1930s motor courts tended to have regionally themed designs, often in the pueblo-revival or Spanish colonial–revival (mission) styles. In some instances, regional references strayed out of the region they belonged to. The St. Francis Hotel Courts in Mobile, Alabama, resembled the Alamo in San Antonio, Texas, as did the Lakeview Courts near Oklahoma City on Route 66. On the other hand, the Alamo Court and Davy Crockett Restaurant in Walnut Ridge, Arkansas, was clad in red brick and looked like a strip shopping plaza. One entrepreneur went as far as to build an adobe-style motel on U.S. 11 in Wytheville, Virginia, and a similar structure in nearby Radford, Virginia. The purpose of vernacular road-related America was not to express historical or geographic accuracy but simply to use any means necessary to fascinate motorists enough so that they would stop and spend money.

A number of cabins, such as Frank Redford's famous 1935 Horse Cave, Kentucky, motel called the "Wigwam Village" where each cabin resembled a large, freestanding teepee, took unique shapes. He built a second motel in nearby Cave City in 1937 (figure 4A).[75] Eventually, Redford built seven Wigwam Villages including two on Route 66, one in Holbrook, Arizona, in 1949 (figure 4B) and one in Rialto, California. The teepees at these establishments measured around thirty feet high, twenty feet in diameter, and were made of reinforced concrete.[76]

As roadside businesses flourished and took on new forms, individual states continued to promote Highway 66 as a tourist route to attract motorists. For example, the New Mexico state government actively sought auto tourists by advertising in at least twenty-three nationally distributed periodicals in the 1930s and by setting up visitor centers staffed with trained personnel where major highways crossed its borders. Like the railroads, the state of New Mexico distributed postcards and brochures throughout the United States. Beginning in

FIGURE 4A AND 4B. Redford's Wigwam Village in Cave City, Kentucky, built in 1937 (above). Photo by author, December 1997. A similar wigwam motel on Route 66 in Holbrook, Arizona, built in 1949 (below). Photo by Sharon Vaughan, October 1998. Note vintage 1950s cars.

1931, New Mexico issued a free state road map to tourists, and by the late 1930s, these maps had color illustrations depicting spectacular scenery, cowboys, and Native Americans. New Mexico began placing picturesque historical markers beside its highways in 1937.[77]

State governments and other promoters such as the U.S. Highway 66 Association worked to link Route 66 with the lore of the Southwest. In 1938 the association added the title "the Will Rogers Highway" to Route 66 to identify the road with the famous cowboy who had died in 1935 and promote the highway as a tourist route. A late 1930s linen postcard of the Laguna Pueblo issued by the Southwest Post Card Company featured a colorful, idealized drawing of two Pueblo women carrying large pots on their heads (plate 6). A caption on the reverse reads, "Laguna is one of the very picturesque Indian villages on Route 66—the Ocean to Ocean [sic] route. . . . [T]he women make pottery of a very attractive design." Another postcard of the same period depicted the modern, paved highway winding through New Mexico mountains and described Route 66 as "the highway [that] winds through the scenic Sandia Mountains. . . . Picturesque little Spanish villages dot the landscape at frequent intervals adding interest to the scene."[78]

The United States economy gradually recovered in the late 1930s and sprang to life with the nation's entry into World War II in December 1941. The booming war economy actually suppressed tourism on Route 66 because most people either went to war or were busy working, and the U.S. government rationed many resources, especially gasoline and tires. National concentration on the war effort temporarily halted promotions of Route 66, and the highway took on a utilitarian and strategic role.

Sporadic investment in Route 66 and other highways continued during the war because businessmen and officials realized that having all-weather, long-distance roads with amenities such as gas stations and motels was important for the war effort. Despite this, Route 66 deteriorated. Studies by the Public Roads Administration during 1941, 1942, and 1943 indicated that more than 50 percent of all defense materials were shipped by truck instead of rail. These trucks usually exceeded prewar weight limits and that's because truckers were able to successfully pressure states into overlooking truck limits by appealing to patriotism.[79] Military convoys transporting arms and troops westward jammed Highway 66.

Trucks carrying military supplies were exempt from rationing and took to the roads in great numbers. With fewer motorists paying the gasoline taxes required to build and maintain highways, and with increasing numbers of heavy trucks and convoys traveling Route 66, ruts formed in pavement that contractors had often laid thin in the 1930s in an effort to pave the entire route quickly. Some stretches of Route 66 in Illinois became so broken up they were nearly impassable. In 1943, the federal government allocated money to build new, twenty-four-foot-wide concrete sections alongside the existing roadway in some areas, leaving a sod median. This allowed motorists to continue using the original pavement during construction. These segments formed parts of a proposed divided highway from Chicago to St. Louis, authorized by the Defense Highway Act of 1941.[80] The retired operator of an Illinois Route 66 restaurant described Route 66 during this time as "the military highway that they made four-lane all through Illinois."[81] These wartime alignments are still visible and are partly in use today, although they have been bypassed by Interstate 55.[82]

Between 1941 and 1945, the United States invested over seventy billion in war-related capital projects in California alone. This created jobs for over five hundred thousand men and women in the Golden State.[83] The Okies' inflated expectations of prosperity in California became reality less than a decade after the Dust Bowl ended. Most of the millions of workers who flocked to industrial centers in the West and Midwest migrated in their private automobiles on Route 66 and other long-distance highways.

Although private automobile production dropped from about 3.8 million in 1941 to a mere 650 in 1942, and the federal government rationed gasoline, tires, replacement parts and oil, motorists continued to use Route 66 but rarely for tourism. During the war, one Route 66 gas station in Oklahoma repaired motorists' cars with parts salvaged from disabled cars, some of which Dust Bowl migrants had abandoned only a few years earlier.[84]

When the war ended in 1945, Route 66 sat in a state of disrepair; however, within months of the war's end, the road sprang back to life. Migrating people—for example, veterans seeking employment in California—clogged the damaged road, and others took long-postponed family vacations. People who had moved to California from Oklahoma and neighboring states either returned to Oklahoma after they had made money working in the defense industries in California or continued to live and work in California or other western states and traveled Route 66 to visit relatives back home.[85] Although road crews rushed to repair the highway, years passed before it was free of the damage caused by war-related traffic.

In the years immediately following World War II, more than 8 million Americans migrated to the West, and 3.5 million settled in California.[86] Traffic counts near Tucumcari, New Mexico, steadily increased after a severe dip during the war, and the percentage of out-of-state cars crossing into it also continued to increase. In 1941 an average of 1,359 vehicles passed on Route 66 in Tucumcari each day, 54 percent of which were from out-of-state. In 1944 that figure was 874, 54 percent of which were from out-of-state. The figures for 1950 and 1955 were 2,137 and 70 percent and 3,308 and 73 percent, respectively.[87]

Route 66 began its rise to fame in the decade following the Second World War. In 1946 Jack D. Rittenhouse traveled its entire length in a 1939 American Bantam coupe so he would be able to write a "mile by mile complete handbook" of Route 66. Rittenhouse captured the spirit of postwar Route 66 when he wrote, "Well, you're on your way—over two thousand miles of fascinating highway ahead of you. One of life's biggest thrills is the realization that we're on our way."[88] Rittenhouse's book gave the mileage between Route 66 towns as well as the locations of natural and historic attractions, tourist courts, restaurants, souvenir shops, and gasoline stations. The book included small maps and featured a series of miniature pen illustrations with regional themes such as skyscrapers for Chicago, a tractor for Funk's Grove, Illinois, Will Rogers and his lasso for Claremore, Oklahoma, a cowboy riding a horse for the Texas Panhandle, an Indian smoking a pipe for San Fidel, New Mexico, and the Grand Canyon for Arizona.[89] The pictures took readers on a journey of regional motifs from the plains of Illinois to the beaches of Los Angeles. These symbols represented the regions that Route 66 crossed and expressed tourist expectations about what it would be like to travel the highway, which dated back to the railroad era.

In 1946, the same year Rittenhouse's book was published, songwriter Bobby Troup set out on Route 66 for a ten-day trip from Pennsylvania to California. Although he called Route 66 "possibly the worst road I've ever taken in my life," he enjoyed traveling it.[90] While he and his first wife, Cynthia, were staying at a tourist court on Route 66, she suggested the title for a new song, "Get your Kicks on Route

66," and he wrote the tune. The song was a "lyrical travelogue of the road," which Nat King Cole recorded that same year and soon became the theme song of the highway and helped popularize it.[91]

Road-related businesses that had survived the war prospered, and new enterprises sprang up along the ever-expanding roadside strips near cities and towns. These new businesses were often family-owned and similar in management and relationship to the road as prewar businesses, although their number increased dramatically. A government survey of tourist camps showed that New Mexico had 213 such camps in 1935, all of which were owner-operated. A similar survey in 1948 counted 537 motels, of which 527 were owner-operated. Most pre-1950 courts and motels had between seven and twenty units.[92] Motel numbers in neighboring Route 66 states expanded as well. According to the 1950 Bureau of Census Report on Courts, Arizona had 370 tourist courts in 1939 and 704 courts and motels in 1948.[93]

With the exception of the often-standardized designs of franchise gas stations, most road-related buildings were still vernacular and unique in the decade after the Second World War. Many roadside entrepreneurs acted as their own contractors and designed their own buildings along the growing automobile strips.[94]

As culture and technology changed, motels evolved along with them. In the late 1940s, tourist court and motel cabins generally became more substantial and offered more amenities, especially in the West.[95] Motel builders began to abandon the cabin design in the early 1950s in favor of connected units. "Classic motels" were more economical to build, more durable, and allowed motel operators to better monitor their guests. By this time, the majority of the motel industry was beginning to target the "hotel-class" customer.[96] Many of the more adventurous or bohemian tourists who had once auto camped no longer stayed at motels, but rather bought camper trailers or tents and backpacks and camped at private campgrounds or at state and national parks. Auto travel and roadside accommodations no longer represented a rugged, strenuous life close to nature. The primary focus of a motel room had become the big comfortable double, queen, or king-sized bed with a radio and, by the 1950s, air conditioning and a television.[97]

The 1950s "classic motel," with its joined units under one large roof, generally consisted of a standardized building with large signs and fancy names designed to connote the same regional, exotic, or domestic themes that many of the earlier tourist courts had tried to communicate with architecture. On Route 66 names evocative of Spanish haciendas, such as the El Vado Motel, and southwestern pueblos, such as the Zia Lodge, were often used.

In the 1950s, the number of figural signs and road-related buildings increased as promoters espoused the wonders of Route 66, especially in its southwestern portion. A postcard dated 1954 continued the effort begun in the 1930s to link Route 66 to the image of the Southwest as a "land of enchantment" and exploit the region's exotic history. The face of the postcard showed Albuquerque's Central Avenue including the facade of the Alvarado Hotel (a Harvey House on Route 66). The card's caption reads:

> U.S. Highway 66 [is] one of the finest highways in the nation. It is certainly one of the most historic roads in all of America for possibly at this very point the Conquistadors may have passed on their way to Santa Fe, the wagon trains of early settlers, Indian raiding parties or the protecting troops of soldiers, all may have played their small part in the eventual creation of the Central Avenue of today.[98]

This caption is highly reminiscent of the railroad promotions of the early twentieth-century and demonstrates the relationship between the marketing strategies of the railroads and those of the promoters of Route 66.

A significant component of the Route 66 landscape of the 1950s was the billboards that advertised road-related businesses. Although many localities had zoned against billboards in previous decades, businesspeople built them anyway and officials often let them stand because they brought more business into town. Certain establishments, such as the Club Cafe in Santa Rosa, New Mexico, and the Cliff Dwelling Trading Post on the Arizona-New Mexico border, posted billboards for miles and miles along the highway in each direction. The Club Cafe used its distinctive "fat man" character as a logo, and the Cliff Dwelling Trading Post utilized derivatives of stereotyped Native Americans developed in the preautomobile era. Ron Chavez, owner-operator of the Club Cafe and inventor of the fat man logo, fought an extended court battle with the federal government to keep his billboards on Route 66 after the Johnson Administration passed the Highway Beautification Act in the late 1960s.[99]

Billboards highlighted businesses that motorists might otherwise miss. Isolated establishments that sold gas, food, souvenirs, or a room for the night depended on billboards to announce their presence ahead. Sometimes the billboards promised a sensational exhibit, such as a two-headed cow or a pit of rattlesnakes, to lure vacationers into stopping. The Foutz Grocery between Laguna and Albuquerque featured a live, tame bear that would remove the cap of sodas with its teeth for amazed tourists.[100] Businesses often advertised "real Indian crafts," Navajo rugs, and sometimes "real Indians" (plate 7).

The themes that road-related businesses used to draw visitors echoed those used by the railroads. Stereotypical images of Native Americans proliferated along Route 66 (figure 5). In Two Guns, Arizona, tourists stopped to see the site of an alleged 1878 battle between Navajos and Apaches in which a Navajo war party supposedly pinned a group of about forty Apaches in a cave and killed them.[101] In 1925, Two Guns became a tourist trap operated by Harry E. Miller, a Native American veteran of the Spanish American War who used the alias "Chief Crazy Thunder," where predominately white tourists visited the "Apache Death Cave," saw a zoo with mountain lions, Gila Monsters, and coral snakes, toured a phony Indian cliff dwelling, and perused an assortment of Indian curios.[102]

In nearby Winslow, Arizona, tourists stopped under a twenty-foot-tall painted Indian to buy "Indian Jewelry, Moccasins, and Western Curios," as store signage put it, at Joseph Joe's Big Indian Store. Not far away, in a direct copy of Fred Harvey promotions, Ray Meany built his "fabulous" Hopi House. Meany constructed his building of adobe, and it featured pueblo-revival flat roofs and exposed roof timber ends (vigas). Meany's Hopi House offered "Curios, a Motel, Rugs, Mineral Rocks, Beer & Wine, a Cafe, a Texaco station, and an Indian Trading Post."[103] Queenan's Trading Post, which sold Indian souvenirs in Elk City, Oklahoma, and was designed in the pueblo-revival style, had a colorful fifteen-foot-tall kachina doll named "Myrtle" beside the parking lot.[104] This mix of businesses created a vernacular, linear cultural landscape of a highway dotted by ethnic and regionally themed retail establishments and attractions that were housed in unmatched commercial buildings with whimsical, often figural thematic signs.

The U.S. Highway 66 Association continued to push Route 66 and utilized much of the same imagery and clichéd icons that had been used to promote the highway in earlier decades. In 1947 Ralph Jones, a New Mexico motel owner, addressed the postwar reorganization meeting of the U.S. Highway 66 Association in Oklahoma City. He said, "My friends, just because you live here among them all, do not lose sight of the fact that there are literally thousands of travelers who have never seen an Indian. Indians have tremendous pulling power. And don't forget the value of the cowboy, either."[105]

Efforts made by the governments of Route 66 states to promote auto tourism often relied heavily on Spanish history and Native American cultures. A 1954 official New Mexico road map featured a drawing of a conquistador in armor riding a horse, sketches of Indians and Indian-made artifacts, three photographs of Indian ruins, and several pictures of Spanish missions along with a Route 66 shield. The map's cover featured three Native American dancers in full regalia.

Similarly, the 1958 official highway map of Oklahoma had depictions of traditional Indians standing beside cowboys as well as flattering portraits of modern highways. In an address printed on the map, then Oklahoma governor Raymond Gary wrote, "You will find our people friendly and eager to please. You will also find historic Indian settlements, cowboy lore, and the reality of the Old West, as well as the more modern vacation pleasures." The map also states proudly, "Oklahoma is doing its part in connecting the nation with the new super interstate Highways."[106] This advertising attempted to portray Route 66 states as offering auto tourists a genuine historical experience but at the same time tried to assure potential tourists that while their state was interesting, it was not a scary rural backwater. In the future-oriented 1950s, having a rich history was not enough: a state had to prove its allegiance with the cult of progress and modernization to prove itself a worthy destination for the American traveler.

While southwestern state governments focused on heritage tourism, Route 66 businesses along the entire route relied on abstractions of regional cultural icons to get tourists to stop. In addition to the two Wigwam Motels on Route 66, pueblo-revival style motor courts appeared on Route 66 from Oklahoma to Arizona. These hostelries usually had ethnically suggestive names such as the Zuni Motor Lodge, the El Don Motel, the Pueblo Bonito Court, the El Sueno Motor Court (plate 8), and the aforementioned Zia Lodge and El Vado Motel.

FIGURE 5. Tee Pee Trading Post built ca. 1940,
Tucumcari, New Mexico. Photo by author, August 2003.

The Zuni Motor Lodge, a mock pueblo complete with wooden lad-
ders and a lookout tower (plate 9), claimed to be "one of the finest and
most unique lodges in the Southwest. Of the Spanish-Indian architecture offering every comfort and service to the seasoned traveler."[107] The
motel used language similar to that created by promoters to describe
Fred Harvey railroad hotels. A postcard issued in the same decade by
Fred Harvey describes the Franciscan Hotel as a "structure typical of

the architecture brought to the Southwest by the early settlers." The caption read, "Every attention is paid to the comfort of cross country tourists, whose prolonged stay in Albuquerque is desirable to all of Albuquerque."[108]

The marketing of Spanish and Indian architecture was not confined to the far West. The Park Plaza Motel, a Spanish colonial–revival motel, which belonged to an early chain, was located on Route 66 in St. Louis. Other Park Plaza motels could be found on Route 66 in Tulsa, Oklahoma, and Amarillo, Texas.[109]

In the 1950s, themes along Route 66 became increasingly fantastic, abstract, and divorced from actual local cultures. Contact with Indian crafts and real Native Americans gave way to symbolic monuments such as the sign at Twin Arrows, Arizona, a trading post and gas station that used two bright-red, thirty-foot-tall arrows beside Highway 66 to entice tourists to stop, eat, and buy gasoline and souvenirs (figure 6), and the Apache Motel. The Cristensens' Cliff Dwellings Trading Post in Lookout Point, New Mexico, was called the Lookout Point Trading Post until the owners changed the name in 1953. The cliff dwellings for which the business was named were actually built as a movie set for the film *Ace in the Hole*, further blurring the line between historical fact on Route 66 and Hollywood fantasy.[110] The symbolic themes of middle and late 1950s roadside promotion continued to speak to the Southwest's Spanish and Mexican heritage.

In Albuquerque, the El Sombrero Restaurant took the form of a giant sombrero that customers entered through the rim.[111] Similarly, patrons of the La Cita Mexican Restaurant in Tucumcari, New Mexico, entered the establishment under a giant sombrero. As if this weren't enough, La Cita's big neon sign is also sombrero shaped, and a mural directly over the door depicts a Mexican in a sombrero leaning listlessly against a giant cactus.

As images of Native Americans and Latinos proliferated along Route 66 in the 1950s, so did those alluding to the "Old" or "Wild West" theme. The cowboy icon appeared on numerous signs on Route 66 west of Missouri. In Tucumcari, New Mexico, the Palomino Motel had a snorting bucking bronco as its sign. The Rio Pecos Ranch Truck Terminal in Santa Rosa had a smiling cowboy driving a truck on its sign. Just off Route 66 in Amarillo, Texas, a giant sign in the shape of a cowboy in a ten-gallon hat announced that motorists had arrived at the Big Texan Steak Ranch.[112] A neon sign in the shape of cowboy

FIGURE 6. Twin Arrows, Arizona. The symbols along Route 66 became increasingly abstract. Photo by author, October 1998.

boot identified the Silver Spur hotel in East Amarillo, and a postcard for the Will Rogers Motor Court in Tulsa, Oklahoma, depicts Rogers on a rearing horse (plate 10). On a tall sign for the Round Up Motel in Claremore, Oklahoma, a neon cowboy blew rings of smoke with his cigar.[113] Like the Cliff Dwellings Trading Post, the cowboy theme was based more on Hollywood than on history. In addition to signs and business logos, several theme parks featuring the "Old West" emerged along the road. One such establishment was Frontier City, U.S.A., created in 1958 by Jimmy Burge, located on Route 66 near Oklahoma City. This tourist attraction featured a mock "western" town complete with a marshal's office, jail, saloon, and train (the Frontier City & Santa Fe), which took "a visitor on an exciting ride through this rough-and-ready town of the 'Old West.' There is always the danger of a train robbery by outlaws in the area."[114]

A Frontier City, U.S.A., postcard from the 1950s depicted a mock battle among robbers, train engineers, and marshals around a bright red tourist train with a miniature steam engine and open cars with red and white striped canopies to shade visitors from the ever present Oklahoma sun (plate 11). Another postcard showed Frontier City marshals subduing an "outlaw" in front of the marshal's office. The attraction also featured a "gunfight corral" where visitors paid twenty-five cents to watch a gun fight while sitting in bleachers purchased from President Eisenhower's second inauguration. It had a "burning covered wagon" at its gate, which smoldered twenty-four hours a day to draw motorists' attention. Fletcher Williams, son of Frontier City partner Jack Williams said: "The wagon was made out of fire-retardant material, but it looked like it had just gone through an Indian attack. People were always stopping to take pictures of it."[115] At Frontier City, tourists could enter the movie set of their favorite western and watch the Hollywood drama unfold in person.

Farther west, Route 66 auto tourists found the privately owned "New Mexico Museum of the Old West" located near Moriarty, forty-five miles east of Albuquerque. The New Mexico Museum of the Old West was little more than a venue in which to buy "Indian crafts" and other trinkets with western themes at the "Indian Trading Post." Before they got back on the busy highway, they could, according to historic postcards, also have a beverage at the "1860 Saloon," and perhaps ogle the fifteen-foot totem poles, ride a "genuine stage coach" with "real horses," see "authentic Longhorn cattle," and watch Indians dance on a decorated outdoor stage. A 1950s postcard (plate 12) claims that weary travelers who took a break from their trip could see "The largest longhorn steer alive with horns measuring 6 feet tip to tip shown in native corral." The reverse side of the same card urged tourists to make the trip soon because, "There are only a few of these hardy critters left—and they soon may become extinct."[116] The promoters of the

New Mexico Museum of the Old West and similar sites portrayed the longhorn, the buffalo, and the Indian as features of Route 66 that were exotic, wonderful, and doomed, much as the Anglo travel literature of the nineteenth century had.

As it turned out, the longhorn, the buffalo, and the Indian outlived Route 66 (figure 7). With the passage of the Interstate Highway Act of 1956, the fate of the narrow, overcrowded highway was sealed, along with many of the independent businesses that lined it. The road-related strip arranged in a linear corridor directly beside the travel lanes proved to be inefficient and dangerous. Route 66 could not handle the ever-increasing volume of high-speed traffic. The vernacular commercial strips had many intersections that endangered travelers and increased driving time within and between cities.

The large numbers of trucks, farm machinery, and slow, local drivers made long-distance travel on the two-lane sections of Route 66 slow and treacherous, and in the 1960s and 1970s, the majority of travelers rejoiced as highway builders bypassed segment after segment of old Route 66 with a modern four-lane divided roadway. The transition from a two-lane, regular-access highway to a four-lane, limited-access road was gradual. Often highway builders constructed a new road alongside the two-lane highway and then opened both sides as a four-lane road.

In the 1960s, the former roadside "wonderland" fantasy became increasingly standardized, regulated, and uniform throughout the nation not only because of the increasing miles of interstates, but also because the franchise system had become widespread. By the late 1960s, corporate images such as McDonald's Golden Arches, created by architects and professional graphic designers, had eclipsed those of independent, family owned businesses like the Club Cafe in Santa Rosa, New Mexico, along American highways. Large corporations did not require eccentric signs and folk sculptures to attract customers. By the 1960s, the use of ethnic imagery, which often had patronizing or even offensive connotations, became less popular. Businesses increasingly utilized abstract signature logos designed primarily for recognition.[117] Designs such as McDonald's mansard roofed restaurants developed in the 1970s acted as advertisements but provided no entertainment as earlier figural architecture often had. Large, lighted signs became so commonplace and tastefully designed that motorists hardly noticed them unless they were searching for a gas station,

FIGURE 7. The Lasso Motel in Tucumcari, New Mexico,
on Route 66. Photo by author, September 1998.

restaurant, or motel. Today, the blocky and familiar yellow-and-black
Waffle House sign is often a welcome sight to hungry travelers but
is certainly not fascinating or unique. Building designs and logos for
businesses, such as the Comfort Inn, Motel 6, and Burger King have
no regional, historical, or ethnic connotations.

Many of the vernacular motels and road-related attractions
were aging in the late 1960s and had lost their charm for visitors

who saw them as run down, even sleazy. Most motorists of the 1960s wanted efficient and standardized amenities. Slick chain restaurants, motels, and gas stations clustered conveniently at exits soon filled this demand.

Ironically, during the 1960s when Route 66 was in decline, the highway enjoyed some of its greatest notoriety. One of the highway's greatest sources of publicity was the television series, *Route 66*. The popular CBS television show, which aired from 1960 to 1964, featured George Maharis and Martin Milner as Tod and Buz, a pair of clean-cut highway adventurers who drove a new Corvette across the West, doing good deeds and teaching moral lessons to locals.[118] The "Route 66 Game," a spin-off of the show, promised that players would "travel the highway to adventure with Tod and Buz." The game featured car-shaped pieces, colorful play money, and a board depicting a stretch of Route 66.[119]

Other manufacturers from the 1960s utilized the name "Route 66" to sell products. An example was Route 66 Premium Table Grapes sold in cans by Suma Fruit International. Manufactured in the early 1960s, the can's label pictured a colorful Route 66 shield crowned with a stem of red grapes and the word "Route" written in stylized chrome lettering. Behind the shield and the lettering, the label portrayed a road lined by lushly fruited grape arbors.[120] Presumably, the grapes of Route 66 were no longer grapes of wrath. Another product carrying the Route 66 name, Route 66 Cigarettes, probably went into production in the 1960s in Germany.[121] The pack has a red and blue Route 66 shield and the brand is apparently still being produced in Poland.[122]

Despite the highway's fame, only the owner-operators of Route 66 businesses and the U.S. Highway 66 Association seemed to mourn the loss of the "Main Street of America." Many businesses moved to the nearest interstate exit or at least put signs along the interstate directing motorists to their establishments.

As the interstates eclipsed Route 66, the U.S. Highway 66 Association staged an all-out effort to associate the name "Route 66" with the new interstate highways (I-55, I-44, I-40, I-15, and I-10) that were gradually replacing the historic road. At first, the association tried to convince the Federal Highway Administration to assign the new interstates with a single designation "Interstate Highway 66." The bureaucrats of the agency refused because such a designation did not conform to their highly standardized national interstate numbering system. Once the association lost that battle, it published pamphlets, guidebooks, and postcards that used both "U.S. 66" and the interstate numbers together. These publications touted Route 66 as the connecting theme of a new multi-interstate route west.[123]

In the 1960s, Route 66 promoters published a foldout postcard called "Here We Are Along Route 66," featuring twelve colorful scenes "along the way." The cover of this publication portrayed a happy young couple driving a red sedan. Around 1970, the same company issued an almost identical fan postcard titled "Here We Are Along U.S. Route 66-Interstate 40," complete with "17 colorful scenes along the way." This card pictured a stagecoach pulled by four horses on its cover with the caption, "A Cowboy Cadillac." Inside, both publications featured familiar Route 66 themes: southwestern scenery (Grand Canyon, Painted Desert, Palo Duro Canyon), Indian pueblos, western Indian craftsmen, and dancers (including "Little Nonnie—Indian Dancer," a boy of about four in full regalia), Will Rogers, longhorn cattle, and the Continental Divide. Both cards contain the same text, including this paragraph:

> Traveling Route 66 in either direction between Los Angeles and Chicago is like taking the high road to adventure. For Route 66 takes you to everything that is romantic and colorful in the Southwest and the Middle west. The sights and scenery are marvelous. . . . [I]n New Mexico there are many tribes of colorful Indians. The prairies of Texas, the great longhorn cattle. Oklahoma, the home of Will Rogers.[124]

By 1971, the U.S. Highway 66 Association had changed its name to the Main Street of America Association. In that year the association published a magazine-like booklet promoting the rapidly disappearing highway. The book exploited every name and advertising gimmick that had been used since 1926 to popularize the road. The association appeared to be using a form of public relations cardiopulmonary resuscitation (CPR) to jolt the highway back to life. The busy cover exclaims:

> US Route 66, SHORTEST and FASTEST YEAR ROUND. 2,200 MILES OF 4 LANE HIGHWAY—DISCOVER AMERICA BY CAR—MAIN STREET OF AMERICA—*BEST* ACROSS THE SCENIC WEST—*'See the U.S.A. the 66 Way!'* THE WILL ROGERS HIGHWAY—THE GRAND CANYON ROUTE.

The five red, white, and blue shields of the interstates that had replaced Route 66 appear at the bottom of the cover.[125]

The brochure touts Route 66 as the "Main Street of America" though at the time most of the new route had already bypassed nearly every main street through which Route 66 had passed. Inside, the booklet offers a pictorial guide for each state, featuring Indians, cowboys, ghost towns, historic sites, and national parks. The book also includes a list of Route 66-associated businesses and booster groups. The 1971 booklet worked to promote the new interstates while exploiting the fame of Route 66. The back page reads, "U.S. 66 is one of the best known highways in the United States. Movies were made along it and books have been written about it. It brings the traveler within easy access of world-famous scenery, National Parks and National Monuments that attract hundreds of thousands of visitors each year."[126]

In spite of these kinds of plugs, traffic along the bypassed stretches of Route 66 decreased dramatically. As a Route 66 merchant put it, "When the interstate came, the traffic just stopped, like that."[127] Many merchants campaigned to get interstate highway exits near their businesses. Only businesses that had signs visible from the interstate continued to attract tourist customers.

Although the Federal Highway Administration worked to make Route 66 extinct in the 1970s and 1980s, Route 66 continued to exist alongside the interstates, until the agency finally decommissioned the route in 1985. Many observers pronounced the famous highway dead when the final segment of Route 66, the main street through Williams, Arizona, was bypassed in 1984.

Route 66 officially existed from 1926, when the federal government designated the route, until 1985, a period of just fifty-nine years. The highway reigned as the premier autoroute between Chicago and Los Angeles for only thirty years between 1926 and 1956, because after 1956, portion after portion was bypassed by interstates.

The vernacular road-related landscapes of Route 66 represent a unique period in American popular culture, dating from the era between the dominance of railroad corporations and the dominance of franchise restaurant and motel corporations and their monolithic corporate logos (although gas stations, such as Phillips 66, tended to be more corporate and uniform in design than other roadside businesses during the Route 66 period). The preinterstate roadside's individualistic entrepreneurs exploited motorist's preconceptions, stereotypes, and expectations to vie for business and created a fantasy of the road. The roadside landscape became highly developed on Route 66, mainly because the southwestern images and references that businesses used in their architecture, signage, and promotion were so prevalent and potent in American popular culture.

With the highway bypassed, the eight state departments of transportation and the Federal Highway Administration attempted to ignore the memory of Route 66, the great road they had created only sixty years earlier. However, as a proprietor of an antique shop on historic Route 66 in Missouri explained even though "when the interstates came everybody wanted nothing more than to get rid of Route 66 . . . ever since they finally did get rid of it, they've been trying to bring it back."[128] Erasing the memory of Route 66 proved impossible, because the old highway had become ingrained in America's memory and identity. Already celebrated in literature, song, and television, Route 66 developed into an idea that would spawn a major magazine, attract thousands of members to Route 66 organizations, and prompt the U.S. Congress to pass two pieces of legislation and allocate ten million dollars to preserve the highway.[129] Soon after people pronounced Route 66 dead at Williams, Arizona, in 1984, its ghost began to rise from the cracked pavement and the rubble of its closed gas stations, tourist courts, and cafés. The highway had not only created a beaten path across the American landscape, but it had also made an indelible impression on the American mind. Route 66 was neither the first long-distance autoroute nor the longest; however, unlike other early U.S. highways, Route 66 enjoyed a distinctive identity from the beginning and gained fame like a rising Hollywood star.

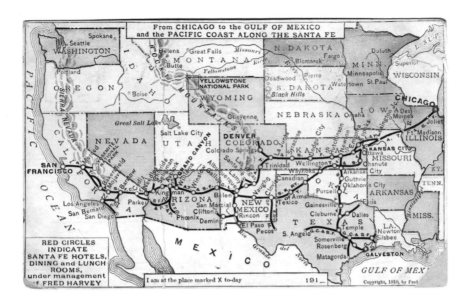

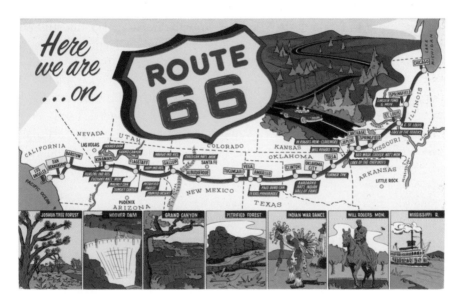

PLATES 1A AND B. Map of Santa Fe lines, ca. 1910 (above). Map of Route 66, ca. 1950 (below). Note the similarity of the routes, especially west of Amarillo, Texas. Historic postcards, author's collection.

PLATE 2. Route 66 in Flagstaff, Arizona, ca. 1955. Route 66 passed right in front of these railroad-era buildings. Note the tracks just visible in the lower left corner. Historic postcard, author's collection.

H.1892   EL NAVAJO, FRED HARVEY HOTEL, GALLUP, NEW MEXICO (AFTER PAINTING BY FRED GEARY)

PLATE 3. El Navajo Fred Harvey Hotel in Gallup, New Mexico, 1942. Built to serve railroad tourists, this hotel also faced Route 66 (foreground). Historic postcard, author's collection.

PLATES 4A AND B. Taos Pueblo, New Mexico (above), and Wright's Trading Post, Albuquerque, New Mexico, ca. 1930 (below), designed by Wright and Morgan Architects. Historic postcards, author's collection.

PLATE 5. Clines Corners, New Mexico in the 1950s.
Historic postcard, author's collection.

PLATE 6. Laguna Indian Pueblo, ca. 1930.
Historic postcard, author's collection.

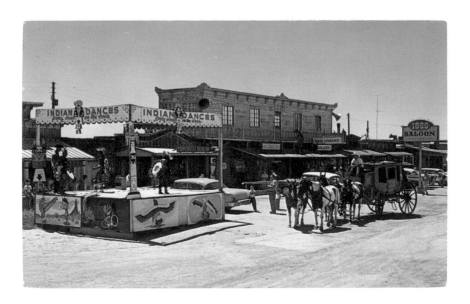

PLATE 7. Indians dancing at Longhorn Ranch and Museum, forty miles east of Albuquerque, New Mexico, on Route 66, ca. 1966. Historic postcard, author's collection.

PLATE 8. El Sueno Motor Court, Claremore, Oklahoma, ca. 1950. Historic postcard, author's collection.

PLATE 9. Zuni Motor Lodge, Albuquerque, New Mexico, 1953.
Historic postcard, author's collection.

PLATE 10. Will Rogers Motor Court, Tulsa, Oklahoma,
ca. 1950. Historic postcard, author's collection.

PLATE 11. Reenacted train robbery at Frontier City, U.S.A. Theme Park in Oklahoma City, Oklahoma, ca. 1960. Historic postcard, author's collection.

PLATE 12. 1950s postcard from the New Mexico Museum of the Old West, Moriarty, New Mexico. Historic postcard, author's collection.

PLATE 13. The Union Bus Depot in Lebanon, Missouri, has lost the characteristics that make it a recognizable historic building. Historic postcard, author's collection. (see also figure 19).

PLATE 14. This postcard, produced by U.S. 66 National Highway Association in the 1950s, used the highway's arched route as an attractive graphic. Note the regional imagery. Historic postcard, author's collection.

CHAPTER THREE

The Fall and Rise of Route 66

Like Route 66, many old U.S. highways functioned as major auto and truck routes, but only Route 66 earned a widespread, international following. Its role as a cultural symbol contributed more to the fame of Route 66 than its significance as an actual highway.

Route 66 had the advantage of passing through the Southwest, a region already made famous by the railroads. However, Route 66 did not gain its place in American popular culture solely because of its association with the Southwest and its cultures; there were three events that were also critical to its canonization: the publication of John Steinbeck's *The Grapes of Wrath* in 1939; the release of Bobby Troup's popular song "Route 66," in 1946; and the airing of the CBS television program, *Route 66*, from 1960 to 1964. The publicity created by these three creative works helped fix Route 66 in the minds of the American people and established the cultural backdrop for the current Route 66 movement.[1] Steinbeck's *The Grapes of Wrath* sold millions of copies. Bobby Troup's "Route 66" song has been recorded by a slew of musicians, including Nat King Cole, Bing Crosby, Bob Dylan, Chuck Berry, the Manhattan Transfer, Van Morrison, the Rolling Stones, Depeche Mode, and Asleep at the Wheel.[2] The television show remained on the air for four seasons, as long as the legendary series *Star Trek*, which aired from 1966 to 1969. Nearly all contemporary Route 66 literature refers to one or more of these three cultural texts.[3] Despite the highway's notoriety, in 1976, the distinctive black-and-white shields that had marked Route 66 for nearly fifty years began to come down. On a cold January day in 1977, state sign hanger John Chesniak helped remove the final Route 66 shield in the state of Illinois and another sign that actually read, "The End of Route 66," which were bolted to a street light pole at the terminus of the highway in Chicago on the corner of Michigan Avenue and Jackson Boulevard. This made a wonderful photo op. As a crowd of highway engineers and other officials watched the sign come down, the group of press paparazzi covering the event proclaimed "the end of Route 66." After Chesniak had unbolted the sign and slowly lowered it, Route 66 made a rapid transformation from a viable highway to a collection of abandoned or little-used sections of deteriorating pavement.[4]

Why did Route 66 cease to function as a cohesive highway while other long-distance U.S. highways such as U.S 40 and U.S. 30 remained relatively intact? The answer can be found in the highway's efficient planning. Since Route 66 followed the shortest practicable route between Chicago and Los Angeles, the corridor became the logical path for the series of new interstate highways authorized by the Interstate Highway Act of 1956 to take its place. Predictably, the longest intact segments of historic Route 66 that exist today, such as the 130-mile stretch that passes through Seligman, Arizona, were sections that deviated from the most efficient route. Most of Highway 66 ended up running adjacent to, or beneath, the five interstates that replaced it. Route 66 fell victim to its own success.

Soon after the Interstate Highway Act authorized the construction of forty-one thousand miles of divided, limited-access highway in 1956, construction began on a vast scale. A vast pool of federal money covered 90 percent of construction costs, with the states financing the remaining 10 percent. The original interstate highway proposal estimated that completing the system would cost about $24.8 billion, however, as one might expect, the project ended up costing somewhat more than predicted. Between 1958 and 1989, the federal government spent a total of $213 billion on interstate highways.[5] Congress designed the original 1956 highway act based on a projection of ninety million registered vehicles by 1975, a number easily reached by 1965.[6]

With so much federal money available, the states were able to construct a national network of highways, creating demand for more cars, which, in turn, increased political pressure for additional highways. This spiraling effect caused the numbers of cars and miles of new highways to explode. Some urban stretches grew to twelve or more lanes wide. As the interstate highways were built throughout the 1960s and 1970s, ever increasing numbers of vehicles jammed the sections of historic Route 66 that had not yet been replaced, filling them with far more traffic than they could handle and thereby making the old unlimited access, two-lane highway obsolete.

In order to accommodate tanks, military convoys, and even intercontinental ballistic missiles carried on truck trailers, highway engineers made interstates four lanes or wider with the traffic directions always divided by a median. These massive roads have no at-grade intersections, and curves sweep gradually, allowing long sight distances. Engineers designed interstates to standards that allowed travel at seventy miles per hour, a speed often exceeded today, especially in the West.[7]

The interstate system, with 42,500 miles of highway, thousands of exits, overpasses, and rest areas, makes up the largest single artifact ever created by humanity. Even if the system had no traffic, billboards, or other services connected with it, the interstate system would have had a tremendous impact on the American landscape. Each mile of interstate highway covers about twenty-four acres of land, with the average interchange consuming about eighty.[8]

The extensive land requirements of highways, such as width, shallow grades, and long visibility lines, made a great deal of mountain blasting and valley fill-ins necessary. The design of interstates was far more intrusive on the landscape than the earlier U.S. highways, such as Route 66. Interstates relate to the landscape differently from earlier highways. They tend to cut through the contours of the land, while most portions of Route 66 followed and conformed to the terrain. The wide shoulders, uniform clear zones, and limited-access entrances and exits of interstates also divide motorists from landscape features. During the 1970s, the vast majority of Americans viewed the interstates as a modern blessing and saw highways like Route 66, as obsolete, dangerous, and inefficient.

In 1984, the Arizona Department of Transportation completed the final bypass of old Route 66 by blasting a broad path through the desiccated hills around Williams, Arizona. Williams's Main Street had served as the last remaining stretch of the "Main Street of America" still in use as a primary highway. On that day, a group of celebrities, including Bobby Troup, gathered in downtown Williams to pronounce the highway dead in a funeral-like ceremony. Troup sang "Route 66," which he had written nearly four decades earlier. During this ceremony, a state highway official whispered to Dennis Lund, the Kaibab National Forest recreation officer, "I don't know why everyone's making such a fuss. Route 66 is like an old can of tuna—once you've used it up, you throw it away."[9] Little did he know how wrong he was.

Like this official, most people probably expected Route 66 to quickly fade from the public memory. In 1985, Route 66 existed only as a series of mostly disused strips of eroding pavement stretching from Chicago to Los Angeles, lined by intermittent clusters of associated commercial structures, more often than not abandoned. Without signs to direct would-be tourists, Route 66 was nothing but a confusing jumble of local, sometimes dead-end, roads and a memory.

With U.S. Highway 66 formally decommissioned, most travelers eagerly took to the new, efficient, and safer interstates. However, after an initial thrill at being able to drive far and fast, a small but ever-growing number of motorists began to long for the "slower pace" of travel on old Route 66.[10] In retrospect, the often crowded, narrow highway with its motley collection of vernacular roadside businesses (most of which were long out of business by 1985) seemed quaint and humanizing compared to the regulated, efficient, and impersonal interstate environment. Motorists found that on an interstate highway, a family could travel from Chicago to Los Angeles and experience very little of the territory through which they passed. Today, many Route 66 fans and commentators contrast the "fascinating" old two-lane road with "bland" new multilane interstates. "By the 1980s, the new Interstate highways replaced the more intimate roads that preceded them. Safer, but less colorful," comments Betsy Malloy in "California for Visitors: Route 66 in the Southwest." The interstates, she goes on, "once prompted commentator Charles Kuralt to comment, 'Thanks to the interstate highway system, it is now possible to travel across the country from coast to coast without seeing anything.' Perhaps it's the desire to 'see something' that keeps Route 66 alive."[11]

In the decade after five interstates (I-55, I-44, I-40, I-15, and I-10), replaced Route 66, the historic highway evolved into an object of nostalgia and soon came to represent the decades in which it was active, particularly the 1930s and the 1950s. Route 66 also began to symbolize concepts such as flight, freedom, the delights of auto tourism, and coming of age to its growing number of fans.[12] Unlike most celebrities, Route 66 rose to fame not during its youthful prime but in old age.

The nostalgic interest in Route 66 that flowered in the 1990s and 2000s evolved out of a series of unrelated articles and personal experiences in the 1970s and 1980s. In 1977, Thomas W. Pew Jr., using interviews of former Dust Bowl migrants conducted by Pew and Terrence Moore, wrote an article outlining the history of the highway that was published in *American Heritage* magazine. He concludes:

No more home-made apple pies, real milk shakes, real coffee; no more place to skinny dip in the Colorado on a hot afternoon, farms with fruit stands run by the youngest kid in the family, advertisements reading 'Chew Mail Pouch' on the sides of barns; no more Burma Shave rhymes, Giant Snake [*sic*] farms, Teepee motels and 'rooms for rent.' Route 66, the Osage Trail, the Wire Road, the mail route, the emigrant road, the Main Street of America, has vanished almost without a trace. The mother road is a ghost road.[13]

Three years later, Pew published an article entitled "Tucumcari Tonight! Requiem for the Last Holdout on Interstate 40" in *American West Magazine*. Pew's title did not refer to "Route 66" but "Interstate 40" instead.[14] In 1984 he wrote another epitaph for Route 66 for *American West* called "Good-bye to Main Street 66, No More Homemade Apple Pie." No matter how many times the Federal Highway Administration and others attempted to pronounce Route 66 dead, interest in the highway simply would not go away. Pew's 1984 article ended with: "Route 66 isn't just a part of America, it is America . . . It's a good road that 66. This traveler, for one, is going to miss her, imperfections and all,"[15] language that foreshadowed the tone of hundreds of narratives one can find on the Internet about Route 66 today.

The activities of individuals and scattered organizations quietly congealed the Route 66 preservation movement through the later half of the 1980s. Tom Teague, a Route 66 advocate from Illinois and author of *Searching for Route 66*, began exploring Route 66 in 1986. He gave up a promotion to take a leave of absence from his job in order to explore and document the people and places of the entire length of the highway.[16] Teague became one of the major proponents of historic Route 66.

In February 1987, about the same time Teague began to take an interest in Route 66, fifteen residents of Arizona, inspired by Angel Delgadillo, a local barber and Route 66 enthusiast, formed the first historic Route 66 preservation organization, the Historic Route 66 Association of Arizona, which remains one of the most active Route 66 groups in the country.[17] Delgadillo operates the popular Route 66 Gift Shop, Museum, and Visitor Center in Seligman, Arizona, and also "successfully lobbied the Arizona Legislature to designate and preserve Route 66 in Arizona as an historic highway" in 1987.[18]

The rise of the Route 66 movement continued at a brisk pace. In 1988, the Kaibab National Forest in Williams, Arizona, began a systematic inventory of remnants of Route 66 within its boundaries and placed seven alignments and structures in the National Register of Historic Places.

In 1989, the University of New Mexico republished Jack Rittenhouse's 1946 *A Guide to Highway 66*, and travelers began to use the book to find remaining motels, cafés, and gas stations, or their ruins, and to seek out the natural sites that Rittenhouse had described decades earlier. In that same year, the Route 66 of Illinois Association and Oklahoma Route 66 Association formed.

In 1990, growing interest in 66 went national when Congress passed the Route 66 Study Act, which authorized the National Park Service to complete a comprehensive study of the entire length of the historic highway and its associated properties.[19] Also in 1990, Michael Wallis published *Route 66: The Mother Road*, one of the most widely read books on Route 66.

In 1993, *Route 66 Magazine* began publication, and in 1994, David Knudson founded the National Route 66 Federation after driving the entire length of the road earlier that same year.[20] In the following year, the Victorville Property Owners Association founded the California Route 66 Museum in Victorville. This museum includes a historic exhibition, a research library, a Route 66 traveler's information center, and a gift shop.[21]

In the middle and late 1990s, interest in Route 66 only increased. In 1995, the National Park Service published the *Special Resource*

Study: Route 66, which had been authorized under the 1990 Route 66 Study Act.[22] And on August 10, 1999, Congress followed up on the previous act by passing Public Law 106-45. This law authorized the Secretary of the Interior to provide assistance to "persons or entities that are willing to participate in the programs authorized under [the] Act" to preserve the Route 66 corridor. The act empowered the secretary "in collaboration with the entities described in subsection (c), to facilitate the development of guidelines and a program of technical assistance and grants that will set priorities for the preservation of the Route 66 corridor."[23] To this end, the act sanctioned the appropriation of ten million dollars in potential matching grants for Route 66-related projects for fiscal years 2000 through 2009. An example of a project funded under this program was the 2002 restoration of the neon sign of the Aztec Motel on historic Route 66 in Albuquerque, New Mexico.[24] The act itself does not state why Route 66 is historically significant, but it references the 1995 National Park Service's *Special Resource Study: Route 66*, which contains a brief statement of significance.[25] The National Park Service Web site describes the importance of Route 66 in these terms:

> Perhaps more than any other American highway, Route 66 symbolized the new optimism that pervaded the nation's postwar economic recovery. For thousands of returning American servicemen and their families, Route 66 represented more than just another highway. "It became," according to one contemporary admirer, "an icon of free-spirited independence linking the United States across the Rocky Mountain divide to the Pacific Ocean." In recent years Route 66 imaginatively documented in prose, song, film, and television has come to represent the essence of the American highway culture to countless motorists who traversed its course during the more than fifty years of its lifetime.[26]

In 2000, members of Route 66 organizations met with representatives from the state historic preservation offices of all of the states that historic Route 66 passes through, except for Kansas and Arizona. One tribal historic preservation officer, representatives from the National Park Service, and the National Trust for Historic Preservation also attended. The purpose of the meeting was to discuss the ramifications and implementation of the ten-year, ten-million-dollar federal initiative. The participants also discussed how best to implement the act.[27]

While most of the professional historic preservationists focused on performing a comprehensive survey of historic alignments and related structures, enthusiasts tended to favor preservation through local efforts—their idea was to promote economic development by increasing tourism and preserving specific Route 66 landmarks. According to Greg Smith, the representative of the Texas State Historic Preservation Office who attended the meeting, Route 66 enthusiasts "proposed incentives to entice more people onto Route 66, including better maps, bigger signs, more museums, and more welcome signs."[28]

Most representatives of Route 66 associations and Route 66 fan clubs favor tourism because of how they view the highway. Enthusiasts see the highway as a cultural icon, whereas professional preservationists tend to view it as a historic artifact made up of significant landscapes and structures in need of cataloging and systematic preservation.[29] To many devotees, the route's symbolic meaning as represented by a limited number of signs and famous sites stands above and beyond the actual historic remnants of the highway as a whole.

As a result of the 1999 federal act and subsequent meetings among enthusiasts and preservation professionals, the National Park Service established the National Route 66 Corridor Preservation Program. The program is "designed as a 'seed,' or stimulus" to spawn more preservation projects along the route by enabling the National Park Service to collaborate "with private property owners; non-profit organizations; and local, state, federal, and tribal governments."[30] In 2004, Michael Cassity completed the *Route 66 Corridor National Historic Context Study*, sponsored by the Route 66 Corridor Preservation Program, which will be discussed further in chapter 5.[31]

Currently, hundreds of fans belong to preservation and promotional Route 66 organizations, including many who do not reside near the road itself. Citizens of foreign countries, mainly in western Europe and Japan, have also taken a keen interest in 66 (figure 8). Enthusiasts from Belgium, Canada, France, Japan, and the Netherlands have formed organizations dedicated to Route 66, and many foreigners travel to the United States to tour portions of the historic highway. Of the 530 visitors who stopped at Angel Delgadillo's Route 66 visitor center in Seligman, Arizona, in early 1999, 208 (39 percent) came from foreign countries.[32] On most days, foreigners, including foreign

FIGURE 8. Many foreign publications on Route 66 came out in the 1980s and 1990s. Photo by author, September 1998.

journalists, can be found milling around Angel's visitor center and the rest of the tiny town of Seligman taking pictures, interviewing locals, and buying souvenirs.

Bill Graves reported in *Trailer Life* meeting two motorcycle riders from France who had air shipped their "hogs" (a kind of motorcycle) to the United States to ride them on Route 66. They "spoke of a huge interest in Europe in America's 'Mother Road.'"[33] When he formed the French Route 66 Association in November 1989, Jean Michel of Paris wrote, "French Route 66 Association is a club of young people, who have two passions in life; the old cars and the road. The Route 66 is like a dream, it represents the road on which we want to drive our old cars."[34]

Naonori Kohira of Japan, who helped create a Japanese version of the movie *The Grapes of Wrath* and who wrote a feature story on Route 66 for a Japanese magazine in 1990, described the reason for Japanese interest in Route 66: "The Japanese traveler wants to come to the U.S.A. and do something different besides go to Disneyland. They want to see and travel old America—the best way to do that, is on old Route 66."[35]

Today, every state through which the road passes has a preservation organization dedicated to saving and interpreting the highway.[36] In addition to these eight statewide groups, the National Historic Route 66 Federation acts as a nationwide Route 66 preservation advocacy organization.[37]

As one travels west through New Mexico and Arizona on the remaining sections of historic Highway 66 today, one can see evidence in the landscape that Route 66 is a popular nostalgic symbol. In Illinois, shop windows in small railroad towns such as Chenoa are filled with Route 66 merchandise. On old Route 66 in the dry prairies of the Texas panhandle, one finds roadside attractions, such as the visitor center and gift shop housed in the recently restored art deco Tower Station and U-Drop Inn in Shamrock, which offer maps, Route 66 merchandise, and friendly conversation. Farther west, entire towns such as Seligman, Arizona, are dedicated to the old highway and host daily busloads of German and Japanese tourists who have come to see what they hope will be the "true" America, unlike the one found in the urban sprawl of American suburbs.

CHAPTER FOUR

Postmodern Nostalgia

Route 66 Has Run Out of Kicks

Cracks so wide you can feel it inside
The sign said go west but we ran out of road
We all rolled in like a tumblin' weed
Old Harleys broken down on one knee
I never thought it could be me . . .
We had a dream but they shot the king
Flag on the ass of my old blue jeans
Tell me tell me
What it all means . . . [1]

These lyrics from the pop-folk group Devonsquare's 1992 song "Bye Bye Route 66" from its CD of the same title describe the romantic decay of Route 66 and the nostalgia it inspires. "Cracks so wide you can feel it inside" seems to eulogize a celebrity highway now tragically gone. The lyrics refer to common Route 66 themes such as the desert West (tumbleweed), vintage Harley Davidson motorcycles, and the hippie movement (flag on the ass). Former glory, faded youth, failed rebellion, and lost innocence all resonate in Devonsquare's words as they do in much of the literature produced about Route 66 since its formal closure in 1985. Much of the contemporary nostalgia surrounding Route 66 concerns a lost decade. For some it's the difficult 1930s, for others the conservative 1950s, while for others, such as Devonsquare, the rebellious 1960s.

The term "nostalgia" was coined in 1688 by Johannes Hofer, a nineteen-year-old Swiss medical student, to describe an extreme case of homesickness, often displayed by wounded soldiers who feared they would die before seeing their homeland again. People could actually die of nostalgia in those days. However, in 1798, philosopher Immanuel Kant observed that people afflicted with nostalgia were often disappointed when they did return home because they weren't actually longing to return to a place, but wished to return to the past, particularly their youth.[2]

Nostalgia remained a diagnosable condition into the late 1800s but increasingly became associated with a general longing for an earlier time.[3] The problem with the desire to relive the past is that unlike going home, it's impossible. Not only can't a person go back in time, but in remembering the past people often create an ideal, the "good ol' days," that never existed in the first place.[4] This infuses the pleasure of remembering with a certain sadness and regret, a helpless sense of loss, which often intensifies as people age. Route 66 inspires every aspect of nostalgia.

Enthusiasts intimately familiar with the historic highway and those who have only a vague notion of what Route 66 actually is associate the highway with a range of nostalgic symbols and experiences. These include the vast deserts of the Southwest, indigenous cultures found along the route (usually ignoring the part of the highway east of Oklahoma), vintage automobiles, patriotism, and the freedom of the open road.

Like most nostalgia, many Route 66 experiences are more imagination than memory. The following passage from a 1995 article about Route 66 published in *Esquire* expresses a number of popular sentiments:

> You find yourself lumbering along a red-dirt road in a totally cherry '55 Cadillac and gazing dreamlike, trancelike [*sic*], out the thick glass windows. Route 66 is way behind you, and the sunset is melting into the car's huge, glossy hood. . . . The desert flatness and its cedar and sage give way to dramatic red buttes and cliffs.[5]

Esquire portrays an almost transcendental experience when describing driving as "gazing dreamlike, trancelike." The depiction of Route 66 as a "red-dirt road" in the late 1950s at a time when its entire length was a busy two- or four-lane paved highway illustrates the unreality of many popular impressions of the route. Similarly, a 1998 tour book, *Route 66: Mainstreet of America*, proclaims,

> The ride from Glenrio is as beautiful and vibrant as a Mexican tapestry—where copper colored cliffs and majestic mesas rise in brilliant contrast to clear desert skies. The roadside communities in this 'Land of Enchantment' are steeped in desert culture, from souvenir shops peddling turquoise and silver trinkets, to ancient Indian Ruins, and lost cities.

This language could have come from a Fred Harvey promotional written seventy years earlier.[6] Many descriptions of Route 66 portray the highway as a place of intense color and contrasts and lost glory—in this case, as a place of "ancient Indian Ruins[] and lost cities."

In addition to representing nostalgic travel experiences and picturesque ruins, Route 66 evokes childhood memories. Virtually every issue of *Route 66 Magazine*, the premier fan periodical, features accounts of childhood experiences on the highway.[7] Most involve recollections of a past decade (usually the 1950s or early 1960s) characterized as a simpler era, a supposedly more honest and innocent time. Many *Route 66 Magazine* contributors express the idea that the 1950s represent an age when life in America was pleasantly free of the complexities and conflicts of today.

In an article entitled "Fifties Memories," published in the fall 1998 edition of *Route 66 Magazine*, writer Bob Moore recalls, "We were respectful of our teachers and tried hard to understand the value of 'X' or the Monroe Doctrine."[8] Moore takes a subtle jab at hip-hop culture when he writes, "A baseball cap was worn with the bill in front—why in the world would you want to turn it around?" "Fifties Memories" also suggests that people were more innocent in that particular decade: "our drugs consisted of St. Joseph Aspirin . . . and cough syrup for a sore throat." The piece ends with a grand finale of unbridled nostalgia: "People had time for themselves and each other and our lives were not consumed with 'stuff.' Bad guys went to jail, always, and good guys got ahead. Everyone respected the President, even if we didn't agree with him. It was a comfortable time in America and some of us miss it very much."[9] It's interesting that Moore chooses the word "comfortable" to describe the 1950s as this may be the ideal term to characterize a white, male, middle-class recollection of the decade before the civil rights movement reached its climax, before the Vietnam War and the protests against it started, and before the women's liberation movement entered mainstream American life.

Nostalgic literature, such as Moore's article, portrays Route 66 as a symbol of a lost era of relative purity and innocence, implying that in the 1950s, Americans had a strong, conservative morality and a wholesome nationalism that most, especially the young, have since lost. In "The Summer of '54," also published in *Route 66 Magazine*, Jim Cook describes his experiences as a member of a group of male teenage friends living near Route 66 in Flagstaff, Arizona, who called themselves "the Joy Boys." Cook describes a "golden summer" of working in garages and hanging around town. One might expect a group of young men left to their own devices to get into trouble, but not these wholesome fellows. Cook painstakingly reassures his readers that while he and his friends longed to hitch a ride to California and ogled tourist girls passing through on Route 66, their exploits remained innocent. Cook writes, "Mark's girlfriend Lynn and her divorced mother Madeline shared an apartment with us. Madeline was something of a party girl, but she also was a steady moral compass for young guys on the loose." Several paragraphs later, Cook describes a relationship he had with a California girl along historic Route 66, once again assuring us of his lack of licentiousness: "We held hands, and necked at drive-in movies, and stumbled around a dance floor or two. We not only didn't get to first base, but weren't sure where the ballpark was."[10] Despite Cook's recollections, most young people, even in the 1950s, must have known "where the ballpark was," even if they chose not to play the game.

Jim Datsko, a regular columnist in *Route 66 Magazine*, takes the supposed innocence of life on Route 66 during the late 1950s and early 1960s to a more abstract and political level. His general thesis in "The Spirit of Route 66" is that the television series, *Route 66*, which aired from 1960 to 1964, represented a wholesome profamily America that the cultural changes in the late 1960s, including "drugs, free sex, race riots, and Viet Nam war [*sic*] riots" destroyed. The author equates the "death" of Route 66 with the end of "values" in America. The article begins, "Growing up in the late 60s was tough. Not only was Route 66 being cut off and left to die a slow death, it seemed as if everything else good in our country was under assault." Datsko continues, "At the same time Route 66 was being 'decommissioned[,]' established traditional values that had developed over millenniums [*sic*], including respect for law and order, were torn down." The article goes on to describe the television series in which Tod and Buz, two "clean-cut heroes," travel the countryside encountering beautiful women and solving "moral dilemmas" for the troubled people they meet.[11]

Very little of the series actually took place on Route 66, but to Datsko, the highway and the television show represent a lost, two-lane American morality. The connection he draws between traditional values and Route 66 in the narrative reaches the surreal when he asks, "Is it mere coincidence that the Bible has 66 books? Or that the tribe of Israel, God's chosen people numbered exactly 66 when entering Egypt?" Apparently, Datsko considers the digits "66" to have a sacred, numerological quality that transcends the Federal Highway Administration's 1926 highway numbering system. He equates Route 66 and the television program by the same name with a good old-fashioned American morality that was torn down by the same faceless intellectual elites who caused the unrest in the late 1960s and created the interstates. He speculates that the good old days are not forgotten and might even be resurrected if we would just preserve the memory of Route 66 and bring Tod and Buz back to the screen. He writes: "Many of us believe the current deterioration of the values that made America great would be reversed by airing this great series."[12] In keeping with Datsko's enthusiasm for the show, starting with its fall 2003, issue, *Route 66 Magazine* chronicled all 116 hour-long episodes aired on CBS between 1960 and 1964 and described of each episode.[13]

The assumption that the 1950s were a more moral and simpler time is widely expressed in Route 66 nostalgia literature; however, a closer look at that decade reveals a different picture. Unlike *Route 66 Magazine* writer Bob Moore's assertion that people were less materialistic or less "concerned with stuff" in the 1950s, Karal Ann Marling's study of that decade, *As Seen on TV*, describes the era as one obsessed with consumer goods. She argues that Americans in the 1950s became fascinated with "shiny new kitchens with pass-throughs from which the TV set could always be glimpsed."[14] Marling asserts that American culture in the 1950s centered on acquiring and using the new products available in the postwar industrial boom and that the 1950s represent a period in which Americans aspired to a "densely material world."[15] The 1950s marked the first true period of economic abundance and prosperity for Americans since 1929. This prosperity, combined with advancing technology and increased marketing, provided a standard of living that few Americans had known.

Many segments of American society, such as African Americans, Latinos, and the Beat Generation rebels, did not achieve the level of prosperity that the white middle-class did in the 1950s, but, at the very least, Marling's study indicates that the majority of people in the 1950s were as interested in material gain as people are today.

The 1950s were a challenging and revolutionary decade in which long-held views and practices began to be challenged, and the world came under new threats, especially from the development of nuclear weapons in the Cold War.[16] Route 66 nostalgia for the 1950s rarely addresses sexuality, racial segregation, or the Cold War.

Traditional assumptions about sexuality were publicly challenged in 1948, when Alfred Kinsey published the results of his extensive study on human sexuality in *Sexual Behavior in the Human Male*. In 1953 he published *Sexual Behavior in the Human Female*, based on a related study. The Kinsey Report remained controversial throughout the 1950s because it showed for the first time that many adults regularly engaged in activities considered taboo at the time.[17]

The civil rights movement gradually gathered momentum in the 1950s, especially after the U.S. Supreme Court outlawed segregation in public schools in its *Brown v. Board of Education* ruling of 1954. However, despite some gains, segregation remained in practice in many regions of the United States throughout the decade and wasn't successfully challenged until the mid-1960s. Segregation, and the conflict and mistrust it caused, was a significant part of life in the 1950s, especially in the South.[18]

The early 1950s also saw the rise of Senator Joseph McCarthy's campaign to spread fear for political gain by accusing individuals, first in the Truman administration and later from many walks of life, including actors and actresses in Hollywood, of being part of a domestic communist conspiracy. This campaign ruined many careers and created an atmosphere of suspicion and dread. Although the hearings that were aired for five weeks in the spring of 1954 exposed McCarthy for what he was, it wasn't until December of the year that his activities were finally condemned by the Senate. McCarthyism flourished during the Korean War, which lasted from June 1950 to June 1953 and resulted in 33,995 American deaths.[19]

International conflict and assaults on Americans' sense of security did not stop with McCarthy or the Korean War. In 1952 the United States tested its first hydrogen bomb named "Big Mike," a ten-megaton monster that obliterated Elugelab in the Marshall Islands. In 1954, the Soviet Union, by then the sworn enemy of the United States, successfully detonated its own hydrogen bomb, and both superpowers, vowing massive retaliation in response to any direct attack, rapidly developed intercontinental ballistic missiles capable of immense destruction.[20] In 1956, then-Soviet Premier Nikita Khrushchev told the West, "History is on our side. We will bury you."[21] In that same year, the Soviets brutally crushed the democratic Hungarian revolution. In 1957, the Gaither Report was released, which assessed the offensive nuclear capability and civil defenses of the United States and the Soviet Union. The report concluded that civil defense preparations in the U.S.S.R. were ahead of those in the United States. By the late 1950s, the Eisenhower administration was actively promoting the construction of fallout shelters as part of the civil defense program, and from 1958 on, the Office of Civil Defense published manuals on how to build home fallout shelters.[22] Individuals built many such shelters across the nation. The Cold War continued into the 1960s, culminating in near all-out war during the 1962 Cuban Missile Crisis.[23]

The families that took their vacations on Route 66 in the 1950s clearly did not lead the kind of carefree lives in an innocent and conflict-free America that many *Route 66 Magazine* and other nostalgia writers portray. Perhaps one reason trips on the highway were so memorable is because traveling across the prairies, mountains, and deserts of the Southwest provided a temporary escape from the anxieties and pressures of life during that difficult decade.

Nostalgic memories are stable and dependable because the past has a certain familiarity. We all know that nuclear war didn't happen, and we may find the other insecurities and problems of the period, such as segregation and racism, easy to forget. Current problems seem far more baffling because no one knows how or if they'll be resolved, making the issues of the past seem more manageable. This makes it easy to view Route 66 as a static symbol, when it was actually a dynamic and evolving transportation corridor during decades that were at least as challenging and difficult as our own.

Although contemporary Route 66 enthusiasts appear to be overwhelmingly white and middle class, they come from various political backgrounds. Consequently, some popular nostalgia writers offer alternative interpretations of the meanings of Route 66 and of the past in general. In July 2003 well-known writer and Route 66 enthusiast Michael Wallis described the Route 66 experience in a different light. In a speech delivered at the Second Annual International Route 66 Roadie Gathering in Tucumcari, New Mexico, Wallis said:

> It was never an idyllic journey on Route 66. Our highway may have earned the title "mother road," thanks to Mister Steinbeck, but sometimes—and too often—she could be an abusive mother. . . . Ask the hordes of Okies and Arkies. . . . [T]he unemployed city workers who were billy-clubbed, spat upon, cursed, abused, cheated, and lied to [and] . . . African Americans, Hispanics, [and] American Indians . . . would not be able to check into even a modest tourist court or dine in a greasy spoon on the mother road.[24]

Wallis, who wrote the up-beat, popular book, *Route 66: The Mother Road*, surprised many attendees at the Roadie Gathering in Tucumcari when he continued:

> As a boy I saw the "no colored" signs at gas stations on my Route 66. . . . I also saw signs declaring "No dogs, no Indians," and only yards away a Native American craftsman sold his hand-fashioned art on the sidewalk. Black families . . . didn't get their kicks on Route 66. . . . Injustice, racism, and sexism in this nation and along this highway are nothing new. All you need to do is read some history to see how it has been nurtured.[25]

In this talk, Wallis broke ranks with many enthusiasts by openly discussing the many hardships that members of ethnic minorities suffered along the road. Wallis publicly recognized that the hardships faced on the highway by "African Americans, Hispanics, [and] American Indians" were as bad, if not worse, than the tribulations of the mostly white Okies. In "Route 66: All American Road," published in the magazine *Route 66 New Mexico,* Wallis writes: "Remember that the highway—our highway—is a true mirror of the nation. Like all roads, this road and what takes place on this road reflects our society and culture."[26]

Other enthusiasts have also deviated from the portrayal of Route 66 as a phenomenon of an innocent 1950s. In "Kerouac & Cassady: Were These Free Spirits the Original Buz & Tod?" published in *Route 66 Magazine,* Lou Delina associates the highway with the defiant hoboism and restless travel of Jack Kerouac and the Beat Generation. He argues that the original Tod and Buz were actually Jack Kerouac and Neal Cassady as Sal Paradise and his friend Dean Moriarty from Kerouac's novel *On the Road.*

In Delina's view, *On the Road* and the "spirit of Route 66" "led to a revolution, a parting of the ways between the old guard and the new progressives, the so-called 'free thinkers.' This movement would manifest itself in the late 1960s." While admitting that the television show "eliminated some of the roguish aspects of Kerouac and Cassady," the "*raison d' étre,* the search for kicks, remains the same." Here, instead of representing traditional American values, Route 66 acts as a pathway for the Beat Generation, eventually leading to the very same cultural revolution of the late 1960s that Datsko and many of his other fellow *Route 66 Magazine* contributors clearly despise.[27]

Although Delina argues that Kerouac and Cassady "were motivated by Route 66," *On the Road* only mentions Route 66 in passing. On his hobo journey west across the country, Kerouac originally intended to take U.S. Route 6 from Bear Mountain just north of New York City to Ely, Nevada, and then find another route over to San Francisco.[28] However, after being soaked by rain and finding it impossible to get a ride in Bear Mountain, he took refuge in an "abandoned cute English-Style filling station" and gave up his "stupid hearthside idea that it would be wonderful to follow one great red line across America."[29] He ended up hitchhiking west on a number of highways. In one of the few mentions of Route 66 in *On the Road,* Kerouac describes the eccentric characters that he encountered in the Los Angeles of the postwar 1940s. "Wild Negroes with bop caps and goatees came laughing by; then long-haired broken down hipsters straight off Route 66 from New York; then old desert rats, carrying packs and heading for a park bench at the Plaza."[30]

To Kerouac and virtually everyone else in the United States in 1947, Route 66 was only one of several famous U.S. highways. However, because of the pervasive myth of Route 66, Delina and many highway enthusiasts assert that the highway was the focus of nearly every aspect of preinterstate roadside America. In its heyday, Route 66 inspired differing emotions. One observer, architect Frank Lloyd Wright, viewed the highway with disdain. Wright wrote, "Route 66 is a giant chute down which everything loose in this country is sliding into Southern California."[31]

People create nostalgic fantasies based on their perspectives on the present. We alter memory to reinforce our current assumptions and ideas. Since 1985, Route 66 enthusiasts and promoters have created a romantic myth that has transformed the highway into a symbol of America and also made it an effective marketing tool. Similarly, other aspects of American history, such as the Old West, the Alamo massacre, the Civil War, and even the war in Vietnam, have been widely glorified, vilified, and repackaged by various interests in recent decades. In "Remembering Memory," historian John Gillis writes: "At the end of the twentieth-century, memory has become such big business that what is being remembered is overshadowed, becoming less memorable than the commemorations themselves."[32] This can certainly be said of Route 66, a highway that has become more a symbol than a road. Gillis continues, "Today, people shop for memories as they shop for anything else."[33] Many of the monuments on Route 66 that people flock to see, such as the Cadillac Ranch in Amarillo (1974) (figure 9), the Route 66 Diner in Albuquerque (1987), and the Route 66 monument in Tucumcari (1997) (figure 10) did not even exist during the time when the road functioned as a primary transportation route (1926–70).

In *The Mystic Chords of Memory*, historian Michael Kammen writes: "an entrepreneurial mode of selective memory has achieved amazing commercial success, though the price for selective memory has been indiscriminate amnesia."[34] The symbols associated with Route 66, and even the name, have become products marketed by merchants on and off the highway. The symbols and concepts used in marketing are sometimes completely divorced from the actual highway and its history.

An example of this is a marketing program by Kmart utilizing the appeal of Route 66 for a product that has absolutely nothing to do with the highway. In 1998, the Kmart Corporation introduced its Route 66 brand of jeans. As Bob Garfield writing for *Advertising Age* points out, in labeling its brand "Route 66," "Kmart opted to associate itself with an icon conveniently pre-imbued with a sense of romantic independence."[35]

When the Route 66 line of clothes first came out, Kmart aired two television commercials that featured the Route 66 image, both entitled "Tales from Route 66." One commercial, which used saturated colors and styles from the 1960s, portrays the urban legend about a cement truck driver who sees a new convertible parked in his driveway and spots a handsome young man in the kitchen talking to his wife and thinks that she's having an affair. A voice-over tells viewers, "So, he backs up his truck, full load of wet cement mix right down the chute," and the audience knows that cement has filled the car. Then the wife and the young man walk outside. "Honey," she says, "this is the car dealer. He just dropped off your birthday present. Surprise!" Then the audio plays "Get your kicks on Route 66," and a title card reads, "Route 66 Jeans. Clothes. It's not Main Street."[36]

FIGURE 9. Cadillac Ranch, Amarillo, Texas, a monument to the many interpretations of Route 66. Photo by author, September 1998.

FIGURE 10. Route 66 monument entitled Roadside Attraction, Tucumcari, New Mexico, 1997, designed by Thomas Coffin and commissioned by the Cultural Corridors Public Art on Scenic Highways Project. Recent Route 66 imagery continues the abstraction of auto and western themes that began in the 1950s. Photo by author, October 1998.

Another 1998 Route 66 Jeans commercial portrays a boy and girl on a date in a vintage automobile. Later in the ad, the girl turns out to be a ghost who died years earlier. The Kmart ads exploit Route 66 as a symbol of nostalgia that vaguely relates to old cars and vintage films such as *Psycho* but do not portray anything specific to the highway, such as a Route 66 landmark or even a city or town on the highway. Like the 1960s television show *Route 66*, Route 66 Jeans really have nothing to do with Route 66 itself. The Kmart writers even play on the term the "Main Street of America," long associated with Route 66, by twisting the phrase to suggest that, unlike "Main Street," the jeans have distinction.

More recent Route 66 Jeans commercials at least show the historic highway. A summer 2000 commercial shows a group of teenagers riding in a convertible along historic Route 66. The car soon runs out of gasoline and the passengers have to push the car, providing an ideal opportunity to show that the slim teenagers are wearing Route 66 Jeans. They arrive at a gas station but discover that it is abandoned. A gas tanker goes by and the young people try to flag it down but the driver passes them, leaving them stranded on a little-used highway marked with a Route 66 shield. This advertisement plays on the fact that the Route 66 of today is half-abandoned and utilizes the ghost-road imagery that is so pivotal in most Route 66 nostalgia. The advertisement still does not show any imagery that is unique to Route 66 except the shield. A more recent slogan for the Kmart jeans is "Route 66, in Style Since 1926," clearly referring to the date Route 66 was officially commissioned. This is a fact that must be lost on most consumers, making it almost an inside joke on the part of Kmart's marketers.[37]

Route 66 Jeans had a precedent. In 1990, a Japanese television crew used Route 66 as the location for Japanese commercials for Edwin Jeans, a brand popular in Japan. The producers picked downtown Kingman, Arizona, to film the Route 66 commercial. John Elmore, a Los Angeles producer, cited two reasons for using Route 66 as a marketing tool for Edwin jeans: "Japanese fascination with American culture—in this case Route 66—and a trend in Japanese advertising toward faster-moving American style, television commercials."[38]

The focus of most Route 66 marketing, including Route 66 Jeans, is the shield, developed in 1926 to designate all federal U.S. Highways.[39] Since the 1980s, the Route 66 shield has been used to advertise and adorn many products, most of which are not particularly travel-related. These products include watches, tote bags, tee shirts, mugs, jewelry, area rugs, phone cards, belt buckles, vehicles, plastic salt and peppershakers shaped like old-time gas pumps, and the aforementioned Kmart jeans. In 1988, Yamaha released a motorcycle called the "XV250 Route 66" in an attempt to associate its product with the Route 66 legacy.[40]

A variety of businesses have also used the shield and "Route 66" as a logo or name, such as the Internet company in New Mexico that has the motto "Get Your Clicks on Internet 66" (figure 11). Other businesses on the Route 66 bandwagon include banks; the Great Plains Regional Medical Center in Elk City, Oklahoma; the Route 66 Antique Mall, also in Elk City; the Route 66 miniature golf course in Gray Summit, Missouri; the 66 Bowl in Oklahoma City; Historic Route 66 Central Oklahoma Long Distance phone company; and the Route 66 Music and Pawn Shop in Wilson, Oklahoma.[41]

Route 66 also has a significant presence on the Internet. A search of the phrase "Route 66" performed in May 2006 using the Google search engine yielded approximately 8,010,000 hits, and a search of "historic Route 66" yielded 302,000 hits.[42] By comparison, the name "Elvis Presley" yielded 11,400,000 hits and "Mick Jagger" received only 4,050,000. In contrast, the phrase "Lincoln Highway" received 696,000 hits, "Route 40" garnered 484,000 hits, and "historic Route 40" earned a mere 124 hits. Significantly, Route 40 is still a commissioned U.S. highway, while Route 66 is not, yet Route 66 still steals the show.[43] The number of hits indicates the number of Web sites containing a given phrase at the time the search was done, generally indicating the popularity of the person, place, or idea named in the phrase.

The vast amount of advertising and literature concerning Route 66, both on and off the web, generally falls into the following nostalgic categories: Route 66 as a symbol of a lost America (the "good old days"); Route 66 as a ghost road of working folk and hardy pioneers; Route 66 as a linear amusement park, representative of a time before the interstates when driving was fun; Route 66 as a symbol of freedom

FIGURE 11. Sign for a "dot.com" on Route 66 in Albuquerque, New Mexico. Photo by author, October 1998.

and rootlessness; Route 66 as a focus of local and regional heritage; and Route 66 as a nationalistic symbol.

One of the most common associations with the road, as we have seen, is the idea that it represents a lost, happier and more innocent era in American history—the point of view expressed by the writers for *Route 66 Magazine* discussed earlier. Author Michael Wallis writes that Route 66 is "a symbol of the way the United States used to be," and in 1998, Wallis spoke of Route 66 as "real family values without the buzz words."[44] In *Route 66: The Mother Road*, Wallis writes, "Route 66 means a time before America became generic. . . . America seemed more innocent. Billboards on the highways were legal; hitchhiking was safe. Nobody knew about cholesterol."[45] Apparently, as previously noted, Wallis has amended these idealistic views and now recognizes that racial and social injustices occurred on Route 66 just like everywhere else. Phyllis Evans, who has helped operate the Aztec Motel on Route 66 in Albuquerque for many years, describes contemporary enthusiasm for Route 66 as "an effort to hold onto some of the things from our past . . . [such as] the genuineness of the people here."[46]

Another common theme associated with Route 66 is that the highway represents the independence, freedom, and hardships of "real," "common," or "true Americans." The mass migration of the Okies on Steinbeck's "mother road" certainly strengthens this idea. Greg Harrison, writing for the *American Motorcyclist*, states that "Route 66 was a part of the American Dream. It represented freedom and adventure. Truckers, motorcyclists and even a couple guys in a Corvette convertible on TV took 'the highway that is the best.'"[47] Harrison merges reality with fiction when he adds Tod and Buzz to the list of actual travelers. The Web site of the Route 66 International Association expresses a similar sentiment: "For thousands of returning servicemen and their families, Route 66 represented more than a highway. 'It became,' according to one admirer, 'an icon of free-spirited independence linking the United States across the Rocky Mountain divide to the Pacific Ocean.'"[48] The "Route 66 Tour Guide," a brochure published by the Route 66 Association of Illinois in 1998, describes the road as a "blue collar, mom-and-pop highway . . . [where] the prized American qualities of hardy individualism and grassroots community spirit found a perfect blend. More than just a highway, Route 66 became a touchstone, showing us not only who we were as a country, but who we could be."[49] The Illinois Association brochure does not say why

Route 66 specifically represents grassroots American independence or community. Certainly, independent businesspeople flourished on other major U.S. highways. Small towns and close-knit communities can be found throughout the United States, and other highways functioned as conduits for workers, including the Okies, migrating to the West during the Great Depression and the postwar period.

In addition to characterizing Route 66 as a workingman's highway, nostalgia literature sometimes associates those who traveled the road with the pioneers of yesteryear. The Holbrook, Arizona, Web site offers the following brief history of Route 66: "In the 1930s through the 1950s, the 'frontiersmen' were travelers on Route 66. . . . This narrow strip of asphalt was a symbol of hope for farmers fleeing the dust bowl and soldiers starting a new life after World War II. The highway served as a symbol of adventure for tourists answering the call of the West."[50] In associating historic Route 66 motorists with frontiersmen, the Holbrook Web site links the highway with the wagon trails that preceded it.

To many enthusiasts, Route 66 also represents a lost, preinterstate era in which driving was fun and the highway was a kind of amusement park through the Old West "frontier." Arizona Route 66 enthusiast Angel Deladillo's Internet site republished in an article by Ted Anthony from the Spokane, Washington *Spokesman-Review* that describes Route 66 as "the ultimate road trip." Anthony writes, "Not so long ago, journey mattered as much as destination. Between 1926 and the 1960s, Route 66 was the 'ultimate road trip' through the essence of pioneer spirit—the American frontier."[51]

Jeanene Tiner's introduction to *Route 66: Mainstreet of America* states, "Route 66 was a means of going someplace—with the emphasis on the 'going' as opposed to the 'someplace.' For the first time, travelers embraced the idea that the joy of traveling was not so much in the destination, but in the journey itself."[52] Certainly many travelers enjoyed driving Route 66, but what made Route 66 more exciting than other American highways? As early as 1910, decades before Route 66, hundreds of auto campers took to the crude roads of the day to enjoy the trip itself. In an article in *Travel Holiday* magazine Steve Wilson, a travel writer, expresses the amusement concept: "The drive was half the fun in those days, and highways like Route 66 had the flavor of amusement parks."[53] Anthony's reprinted piece on Angel's Barbershop's Route 66 Web site describes Route 66 as meandering through "Adventureland's undulating hills."[54]

As with many ideas expressed about Route 66, these sentiments are only part of the story. While historic Route 66 did play host to at least thirty distinctive roadside attractions, Wilson and others ignore the hundreds of miles of often barren, arid countryside and congested work-a-day towns between the attractions on this linear "amusement park."[55] Like motorists on today's highways, most people who traveled Route 66 used it because the highway provided the most direct way to get to their destination. If they ended up enjoying the drive itself, this was usually incidental. As related earlier, the Southwest already had a reputation as a tourist destination before 1926, which Route 66 inherited, and this reputation helped draw motorists to the region. When they reached the Southwest, many easterners, whether they wanted to be or not, were introduced to what David Kammer describes as "an otherwise exotic culture to the rest of the U.S., Pueblos and Native Americans, Hispanic culture and unique styles of building and unique landscapes."[56] This introduction to different cultures and scenery probably helped fix Route 66 in the American mind.

Route 66 nostalgia publications, advertisements, and testimonials often promote the theme that Route 66 gave travelers an opportunity to taste the freedom and openness of the road, the delightful sensation of "going somewhere." Writer Michael Wallis calls Route 66 "the free road."[57] To a longtime restaurant operator on Route 66 in Illinois who has worked beside the highway for over fifty years, Route 66 symbolizes "adventure."[58] Professional historic preservationist and Route 66 enthusiast David Kammer describes Route 66 as a road that "comes to represent travel and freedom in the individual's automobile for all Americans."[59] In this view, the road does not only represent preinterstate travel in the literal sense but also symbolizes the more abstract notion that motorists experienced a heightened level of freedom and release as they drove their private cars down the old two-lane highway. Actually, with areas of heavy traffic through towns and cities, slow trucks, and sharp curves, travel on Route 66 was actually more restrictive in many ways than driving on modern interstates, which offer a continuous passing lane and no sharp curves, allowing motorists to travel at any speed within reason.

To some, Route 66 is a monument to twentieth-century national and local history. Peter Fish writes in *Sunset* magazine, "There are paths that run not just across the American landscape but across the American mind, and Route 66 is among the most resonant of these." He continues, "It became the symbol of American momentum. Everyone's family traveled it."[60] Tom Snyder, founder and former director of the California Route 66 Association, describes the significance of Route 66 in his *Route 66: Traveler's Guide and Roadside Companion*: "US 66 became much more than a highway. For millions who traveled her (and millions more who still want to), the road was transformed from a concrete thoroughfare into a national symbol: a vital life-sign for us all."[61] David Knudson, the executive director of the National Historic Route 66 Federation, characterized the highway as a living remnant of a bygone America: "transportation to excitement, to remembrance—2,400 miles of Williamsburg, but living and breathing."[62]

Martin Mathis, a Swiss tourist, places Route 66 in the history of American popular culture when he characterizes Route 66 on his Web page as, "Everything from hamburgers, motels, Coca-Cola ads, Elvis and James Dean to the wide open land and the straight highways that disappear on the horizon, is in it. Route 66 is like Americana in a nutshell."[63] An elderly volunteer at a history museum on Route 66 in Kansas reported that the Route represents "our heritage," and a motel operator who spent over fifty-seven years on Route 66 describes the highway as a "road of memories."[64] To these observers and others, the Route 66 shield takes its place alongside the flag, the bald eagle, and the Statue of Liberty as an American icon.

While much contemporary commentary on Route 66 ascribes great historical and cultural significance to it, to many motorists who traveled the highway during its heyday, the route was simply the most convenient highway. Notes written on a sample of Route 66 postcards indicate that during the highway's period of historical significance, between 1927 and around 1970, motorists tended to be more interested in the weather, the natural landscape, and how many miles they covered that day than in Route 66 itself. A few praised the motel at which they were staying or a specific tourist attraction such as the Painted Desert or the Grand Canyon, but none describe viewing Route 66 as a symbol of America or experiencing any particular form of road-related freedom.

The most common subject in the sample was the weather.[65] A motorist wrote in 1940 on the back of a Route 66 postcard, "Left Gallup, New Mexico this morning, staying in Needles, CA tonight + by tomorrow night be at the end of our route. Was plenty warm today." From

Joliet, Illinois, a Texan wrote in 1944, "Are O.K. at 1:45 PM—had a nice trip. It is nice and cool here + raining." In 1954 another Texas motorist wrote from Albuquerque, "It is much cooler here."[66] A Missouri motorist wrote on a Broncho Lodge, Amarillo, Texas, postcard in 1964, "Having a grand trip. . . . We have had rain on the desert both going out and coming back." Another motorist, from Lanoner Hills, Maryland, sent this note on a "US 66 Texas" postcard from Shamrock, Texas, in 1967, "We got to Texas about 6:00 AM today. All has gone well so far. It is raining very hard now. . . . We will follow Route 66 through New Mexico + Arizona to Las Vegas. The land here + through Okla. is very flat. Try it sometime."[67]

While many Route 66 motorists enjoyed the scenery they discovered along the way, they apparently took the commercial highway landscapes that they passed through for granted. There were, after all, no interstates (until after 1956), and no massive corporate restaurant and motel chains to contrast the quirky, vernacular commercial structures of Route 66 with. Then, as now, people tended to notice features that they found unusual, primarily the western scenery, which stood out to easterners. "On our way home + staying here tonight . . . We saw Petrified Forest, which is very interesting and Painted Desert today. Had a dust storm -thunder showers + rainbow today, and some fine roads," a motorist wrote from the Painted Desert back home to New York in 1961.[68]

This note on a 1953 "Highway 66 Rolla MO" postcard sent to New York State refers to many of the things that Route 66 vacationers typically made note of: "At Merimac Caverns marvelous + several miles deep. Have good weather + car is perfect. Expect to arrive in Tulsa, Okla. before night. Ozarks are beautiful. Stayed in double cabin west of St. Louis last night. Good driving weather. Cloudy but no rain. Girls are fine and enjoying trip. G. is flexing camera. good roads. Best vacation we've ever taken."[69] The writer was clearly interested in natural wonders, weather, good roads, and finding a good cabin to spend the night, but these concerns do not reflect the symbolism discussed by contemporary Route 66 enthusiasts. At least one traveler, who stayed at the Pine Tree Lodge in Gallup in 1957, did not even like the scenery. She wrote, "I'm not much on traveling and this New Mexico and Arizona I don't like."[70]

People living in these "simpler times" seem to have had more worries about problems such as breakdowns and flat tires than contemporary motorists. A 1962 traveler stated, "We are on our way again this AM it is 40 degrees here @ 5:30 AM. We have had a good time + no trouble" on a postcard written at the Forest Motel in Holbrook, Arizona. One stranded couple wrote from Kansas, "slept in car—had bearing trouble with U-Haul." A motorist wrote in 1937 from the Sinclair Pennant Hotel in Rolla, "Dear Verna, We have rain sleet & snow today. E.J. got sick so we stopped at 684 miles."[71] These notes, written in the present by actual Route 66 vacationers, cite specific travel concerns rather than discussing Route 66 as an entity or as an integrated experience. Few motorists traveling west rode Route 66 the entire way but instead often took a series of highways.[72]

Another common concern expressed on postcards was the quality of motel one would find. Without the uniformity of chain management, the quality of motels varied greatly, and people appreciated a good one. "Staying here tonight—cottage 5—nicer than a Hotel," came from Koronado Kourts, Joplin, Missouri, in 1941. Another traveler was happy with his/her accommodations in Springfield, Missouri: "Greetings from a nice trip. Following Duncan Hines led to this beautiful hotel. Had dinner in the crystal room—ah so nice! Kentwood Arms Hotel, 1946."[73]

Once four-lane sections of highway and Interstates began to replace portions of the historic two-lane highway, some motorists celebrated the resulting increase in speed and mobility in notes on the backs of postcards. Mina, a motorist from 1954 drove to Needles through "75 miles of 104 temperature from Kingman here—but on new 4-lane highway." A 1960s driver wrote "Highway 66 is a freeway most of the way!"[74]

One postcard note, from the Delta Motel in Winslow, Arizona, sent to Roanoke, Virginia, in 1964 mentioned encountering the cultures of the Southwest: "There are more Mexicans here than there are white people. The Indians live in stone houses," providing a tiny glimpse into the writer's state of mind and touching on the issue of race on Route 66 so eloquently discussed by Michael Wallis.

Of a sample of sixty used postcards sent during a period ranging from 1930 to 1970 from sites on Route 66, only two mentioned Route 66 at all, and no one wrote "finally seeing Route 66," or "here I am traveling the quintessential American highway."[75] The symbolism and ideals associated with route seem to be recent inventions created since the highway ceased to exist.

However, during the highway's period of significance, some observers did see Route 66 as more than just another highway. One obvious example is John Steinbeck, who wrote *The Grapes of Wrath* in 1939. But Steinbeck wasn't alone. A writer working for the 1941 Work Progress Administration (WPA) *Oklahoma: A Guide to the Sooner State*, took his/her lead from Steinbeck: "Known for many things, Grapes of Wrath families, Cash and Carry[,] Pyle's Bunion Derby, its popular local titles, 'Main Street of America' and the 'Will Rogers Highway of America,' US 66 runs the gamut of hot and cold, mountains and prairies, beauty and sordid ugliness."[76] And of course, Bobby Troup thought enough of Route 66 in 1946 to write his famous song about the highway.

The seeds for the late-twentieth-century Route 66 revival exist in these few sentiments, but most motorists at the time do not appear to have seen Route 66 itself as being particularly significant. When asked by the author what they thought Route 66 symbolized, several people intimately familiar with old Route 66 said that they did not view Route 66 as a symbol or ideal even today. An elderly Illinois restaurant operator simply said that, to him, the highway represented "a living."[77]

From a different perspective, a 1990 edition of the Historic Route 66 Association of Arizona newsletter featured "famed" hobo, "The Man Called John. He says Hobo's [*sic*] like to travel Route 66 because of its closeness to the railroad tracks and 66 caries [*sic*] a lot of history they enjoy."[78] To be close to the railroad tracks is a pretty mundane reason to travel "America's quintessential highway."

In addition to being of secondary importance in most people's minds when it was a primary highway, Route 66 was also dangerous, a fact not often acknowledged in nostalgia literature. A long-time Illinois merchant described the highway as "bloody 66," which she said was a common local name for the highway because of the numerous accidents she and others had witnessed.[79] In *Route 66: Lives on the Road*, Sergeant Chester Henry, who served with the Illinois State Police starting in 1957, describes Route 66 in Illinois, "The intersection of U.S. 24 and 66 in Chenoa was particularly bad. . . . Sixty-six southbound came around a curve approaching the intersection. . . . Route 66 was really a fairly dangerous highway. There were a lot of accidents. When traffic went up to I-55 . . . the traffic danger went down."[80] Similarly, Clyde McCune, a policeman on Route 66 in the 1950s in Arizona saw "quite a number of serious automobile accidents on [it]. . . . You had to be careful. There was enough traffic that if you started to pass, you had better know where you were going and get the passing done before you went head-on into something."[81]

Traveling by automobiles was not as safe in the mid-twentieth century as is it today. According to *West's Encyclopedia of American Law*, in 1965, 50,000 Americans were killed in motor vehicle accidents at a time when the entire population was under 200 million. In the 1960s, automobiles were the leading cause of accidental death in the United States.[82] In contrast, 42,028 Americans died in automobile accidents in 2003 with a total U.S. population of over 281 million.[83] *West's* points out that "Between 1945 and 1995, 2 million people died and about 200 million were injured in auto accidents—many more than were killed and injured in all the wars in the nation's history combined."[84] Bill Pierce, a truck driver on Route 66 in Arizona in the 1950s, describes the section of Route 66 near Seligman: "Once you left Needles and headed for Flagstaff that was a really vicious road. . . . [Y]ou'd come around a curve, and there'd be a disabled car or truck sitting there. . . . That caused a lot of accidents. A lot of drivers at that time would not try to get off the road . . . [and] the roads weren't that wide."[85]

The dangers of auto travel on Route 66 and in the West in general were not lost to popular culture. For example, Jim Morrison's song "Ghost Song" poetically describes a scene that he witnessed on a desert highway around 1947 when he was four years old. "A truck load of Indian workers had either hit another car, or just—I don't know what happened—but there were Indians scattered all over the highway, bleeding to death,"[86] Morrison said. The experience had a strong impact on Morrison, as the many horrendous accidents on Route 66 must have had on countless travelers.

The difference between the ideas and associations expressed by nostalgic literature and the realities of the past shows how people's memory can differ from actual experiences as they were lived. Widespread nostalgia for the decades from the 1930s, the 1950s, and even the war-torn 1940s, when Route 66 was in active use, is an example of how Americans tend to, as historian Michael Frisch puts it, "shrink away from a serious reckoning with their past" by failing to recognize the dangers and difficulties of those decades.[87] Of course the mid-twentieth century had both positive and troubling aspects, but nostalgia writers tend to use Route 66 as a tool to unfairly critique the present.

According to historian David Lowenthal, the difference between history and nostalgic memory is that memory is a personal recollection, while history is a methodical, collective effort to study past events "based on empirical sources." He writes, "We accept memory as a premise of knowledge; we infer history from evidence that includes other people's memories."[88] Most available interpretive materials, such as guidebooks, Web sites, and other literature about Route 66, emphasize personal recollections and do not attempt to analyze those impressions or place them into a wider historical context.[89]

Historians can make generalizations about past events that people at the time could never have made themselves, describing eras, such as "the Renaissance" and the "the Great Depression," that were not yet identified during the periods themselves. As historian Norman Cantor points out in *Inventing the Middle Ages,* a group of early-twentieth-century academic historians actually created the concept of what we consider "medieval." Without much knowledge of ancient Rome and no hint at a coming "Renaissance," people who lived in those times could never have considered themselves participants in a Middle Age.[90] In a similar manner, travelers on Route 66 during the 1940s and 1950s could not compare their experiences on the two-lane highway to driving on four-lane, limited access interstate highways as contemporary enthusiasts often do.

Without a clear understanding of the character of Route 66 during its period of significance, descriptions of what it was like to travel in those days can be misleading. For example, Route 66 nostalgia literature often describes the historic highway as the "open road," a place where motorists could drive without worry or hindrance. "In optimistic post W.W.II America, Route 66 defined a generation looking for adventure and freedom on the open road," writes Guy Randall for a Web site featuring a "virtual tour" of Route 66.[91] Because historic Route 66 is lined with vacant motels, struggling roadside cafés, and roadside ruins, contemporary travelers often experience a vacant, sometimes eerie openness of an empty road (figure 12). However, in most instances, that sense of isolation did not exist when the highway was in full use. In the 1950s, for example, motorists and truckers jammed the highway and patrons filled the restaurants and motels. The open stretches of highway that enthusiasts find today were often filled, when Route 66 was active, with "bumper-to-bumper" traffic that subjected motorists to all of the stresses, dangers, and hardships that accompany traffic jams.[92]

Attempting to understand the character of Route 66 historically by visiting the road today would be similar to trying to interpret the general atmosphere of Manhattan during a weekday rush hour by going there on a Sunday morning. An observer might talk about having a sense of the lonely streets of the city and the freedom to drive wherever one chooses without hindrance or congestion. Author and humorist David Macaulay illustrates a similar methodological error in his 1979 parody of the discovery of Tutankhamen's tomb called *Motel of the Mysteries,* in which archaeologist Howard Carson uncovers remains of the greatest mystery of the twenty-third century, the ancient culture of "Usa," buried in the land mass once known as North America. What Carson thinks is a tomb with a "great altar" and a "sacred fountain" is actually a buried motel room with a television and a toilet.[93]

FIGURE 12. Thirty-eight Pony Bridge on Route 66 over the Canadian River in Oklahoma built in 1933 and photographed in 1998. This bridge has very little traffic today, and one is free to walk around and enjoy the historic structure. However, before the interstates bypassed it, standing here would have been very hazardous. Photo by author, October 1998.

The Cadillac Ranch along Route 66 near Amarillo is an example of the diverse ways in which the sites and symbols associated with Route 66 are interpreted (figure 9). In 1974, Doug Michaels and Hudson Marquez, members of a group of San Francisco architects called the Ant Farm because of their unconventional, underground concepts, built the "ranch." The Cadillac Ranch consists of ten vintage "Cadillacs, ranging from a 1949 Club Coupe to a 1963 Sedan" pointed nose down in a Texas Panhandle wheat field.[94] The designers saw the vintage luxury cars with their tail fins as the ultimate American automobile and Route 66 as the premier American highway.[95] In 1994, Suzanne Gamboa, a reporter for the *Austin American Statesman*, wrote, "To a Yankee, it's a symbol of Texas excess. For Texans, it gives them license to brag about the state's independent streak. Advertisers have used it to symbolize the downturn in the American auto industry. Pop philosophers see it as a graveyard for what they call the American folly of forsaking function for design."[96] The Cadillac Ranch abstractly symbolizes the role of the automobile and highways in American culture, but like many aspects of Route 66, this symbol has been interpreted in numerous, sometimes contradictory, ways.

In recent decades, Route 66 has come to represent a cultural reaction to contemporary late-capitalist America, with its standardized interstate highways and uniform corporate landscapes. Any number of nostalgic individuals associate the old highway with somewhat countercultural products such as Harley Davidsons, leather jackets, and 1950s hot rods; off-beat places such as all-night diners and independently owned motels; and marginal people such as highway drifters, greasers, and bikers (figure 13). For the most part, Route 66's fame is not the result of its association with specific historic events (the Dust Bowl being one significant exception) or individual historic landmarks, but with the ideas that the highway has come to represent in recent decades. A 1997 monument (figure 11) to Route 66 in Tucumcari, New Mexico, which looks like a colossal abstracted chrome tail fin of the type found on 1950s cars, illustrates the importance of nonspecific symbolic imagery in how people perceive Route 66.

Route 66 represents a popular challenge to the contemporary corporate hegemony of road-related restaurant and motel chains, and to federal regulation of auto travel as represented by the interstate highway system. To Route 66 enthusiasts such as Michael Wallis and Angel Delgadillo, the highway symbolizes freedom from the corporate monotony of interstate exchanges and from standardization, control, and regimentation in human relationships. Wallis writes that "Truly a road of phantoms and dreams, 66 is the romance of traveling the open highway."[97] The recent resurgence of Route 66 has, in part, been driven by the memory of a time when (it is believed) travel was not so restricted and practical, when people could wander freely from spectacle to spectacle without fences, infrequent exits, and standardization.

Nostalgic texts often refer old Route 66 as a place where people had time to talk and get to know each other when they traveled. There is certainly some truth to this, as virtually anyone who has traveled historic Route 66 can testify. If one spends much time on the old road and eats at a local restaurant or stays at a historic motel the likelihood that he or she will have an enjoyable and personable conversation with a waiter or waitress, a motel keeper, or a merchant is much higher than if one stays on the interstates. The friendliness one finds on Route 66 does hearken back to a less alienated time; however, there may be some

FIGURE 13. Mock-up from 1950s, Seligman, Arizona. In Seligman, mannequins act out the nostalgic fantasies of twentieth-century auto culture for contemporary tourists. Photo by author, October 1998.

distortion of history even in this, because service people and small business owners were generally more busy during the heyday of Route 66 and may have had less time to chat with customers as they do now.

Enthusiasts often describe Route 66 as the antithesis of interstate highways. An Internet advertisement for the Route 66 Museum in Rancho Cucamonga, California, describes Route 66 as "far more interesting and visually stimulating than following Interstate Highway 40, with its 'superhighway monotony.'"[98] Martin Mathis calls Interstate 40 "the evil road . . . [of] corporate fast food and motel chains" and worked hard to avoid it on his numerous Route 66 trips.[99] Michael Wallis writes, "As one of the old highway's aficionados put it, the opening of the interstates made it possible to drive all the way from Chicago to the Pacific without stopping. The Government called that progress. Thank God, not everyone agreed."[100]

Unlike the interstates, which possess a straightforward practicality, the experience of Route 66 has always involved fantasy and interpretation. Between 1926 and around 1970 on Route 66, few motorists believed that the pueblo-like souvenir stands were actually historic Indian dwellings or that they were even really constructed of adobe, nor did most believe that an actual cowboy would occupy the room next to theirs at the Will Rogers Motel. The image, the suggestion, the reference was enough. In the 1940s and 1950s, many of the sites along Route 66, from "Indian" trading posts, to "pueblo" motels, to "longhorn" ranches, relied on motorists to create their own narratives about what they saw, usually based on their expectations and preconceptions derived from lore about the Southwest promoted by railroads in the early twentieth century, from cowboy literature, and from western genre movies.

Always a matter of pop culture and visual illusions, Route 66 and its mostly faux roadside attractions went against the academic modernist emphasis on honesty in architecture, efficiency, and practicality that characterized the design fields between World War II and 1970, when much of the roadside architecture along Route 66 was built. The popular, vernacular, and built environment of Route 66, as well as of a great deal of nonacademic roadside architecture nationwide, ran counter to prevailing intellectual trends and to the architecture that was being designed by followers of Bahaus-trained purists such as Walter Gropius and Mies Van de Rohe. Although many gas stations were modern in design (usually built from standardized corporate plans), most motels and roadside attractions had historical and cultural themes and were designed and built by locals.

While Route 66 existed during the modern era, historic Route 66 as a nostalgic tourist attraction emerged during the 1980s and 1990s, when postmodernism came to replace modernism as the dominant cultural paradigm. Postmodernism was a reaction against the modern movement both in design and in society as a whole. Modernism aimed to capture the essence of the industrial way of life and create a new purity of thought and aesthetics based on the advance of technology and new modes of analysis provided by science.[101] While modernism involved a progressive search for unity, postmodernism rejected unity, progress, and the existence of an absolute, knowable reality. Where modernism taught a disruption of tradition based on the discovery of universal, technological principles that were supposed to transcend style and fashion, postmodernism emphasized a collage of forms and styles, a fascination with copies and repetition, a rejection of commitment in favor of irony and "pleasure in a play of surfaces."[102] Postmodern theory abandons the modern ideals of the rational and unified in favor of plurality and fragmentation.[103]

Postmodernism, which emerged in the late 1960s but didn't truly take hold in American culture until the 1980s, originated in literary criticism and then spread to architecture and many other aspects of life. Postmodern design created rich and complicated visual imagery in direct contrast to efficient, austere, and rational modern designs, such as Mies van der Rohe's "glass box" skyscrapers and Charles and Ray Eames's functional plywood and fiberglass furniture.[104] Postmodernism in architecture does not simply copy the past; it alludes to it by making often ironic references to past styles and historic landmarks.

In 1977, architect Charles Jencks published *The Language of Post-Modern Architecture*, which heralded the death of modern architecture and the formation of a new movement in architectural design based on historical references. Jencks wrote, "Modern architecture has suffered from elitism. Post-modern architecture is trying to get over that elitism, not by dropping it, but rather by extending the language of architecture in many ways—into the vernacular, towards the tradition and the commercial slang of the street."[105]

In *Learning from Las Vegas*, pioneer postmodern architect Robert

Venturi held up vernacular architecture from the American roadside of the late 1960s as a model of how popular symbolism should play a greater role in the design of architecture. Venturi wanted the academic profession of architecture to move away from the sober and perhaps elitist rationality of modernism and embrace popular culture and embody popular icons.[106] Venturi's thinking clearly paralleled Jencks's. In *From Bauhaus to Our House*, Tom Wolfe writes: "Venturi seemed to be saying it was time to remove architecture from the elite world of the universities, from the compounds, and make it once more familiar to ordinary people."[107]

Instead of turning to technology for the solution to architectural and social problems as the modernists had done, postmodern architects such as Robert Venturi, Philip Johnson, and Michael Graves reused and reinterpreted traditional forms, often using modern materials to do so. As late as 2000, Venturi continued to cite the vernacular garishness of Las Vegas and the commercial strip as examples for academic architecture.[108] The type of imagery and architectural form he championed in Las Vegas could also be found in the historic cafés, motels, and tourist traps of Route 66.

Postmodernism rejects the absolute tenets of modern design such as the "honesty" in the use of materials and replaces it with illusion, allowing stucco to look like adobe, cement like limestone, and marble veneers like marble blocks. This approach has been the modus operandi since the 1920s on Route 66. Builders used materials such as plywood covered with stucco to mimic historic adobe and concrete to mimic the leather walls of teepees without hesitation.

This is not to say that Route 66 was postmodern, but that sites along the corridor possessed elements of mass culture and gave rise to popular metaphors that would later be interpreted in postmodern architecture, as Venturi argues Las Vegas did. Even though most Route 66 enthusiasts are not postmodernist intellectuals who consciously view the highway from a postmodern perspective, the popular images and faux surfaces found on Route 66 appeal to many Route 66 enthusiasts because they live in the postmodern era. Although not architects or literary critics, the public as a whole, including Route 66 enthusiasts, has certainly been influenced by postmodern design and thought. By the 1980s, advertising, movies, public architecture and art, and many modes of public discourse such as the style of reporting the news had been deeply influenced by postmodernism. Postmodernism has so influenced the culture that the movement has altered the way virtually everyone in America sees the world.[109] One simply needs to compare the straightforward and rational television commercials of the 1960s, to the disjointed and surreal advertisements of the 2000s to see how much the popular mindset has changed. Commercials depicting a museum guard feeding French fries to an animated dinosaur skeleton, talking mice in goggles, or a helicopter hoisting a Greek temple portico over the New York skyline would've been very unlikely to inspire the people of the 1950s and 1960s to buy anything but rather would've just been considered weird and confusing.[110] However, the fact that such bizarre images, illusions, and jumbled storylines sell products today indicates that the mindset of the masses has been deeply influenced by the "complexity and contradictions" of postmodernism.[111]

When Route 66 was at it peak (the late 1940s and 1950s), modernism in America was also at its height, and when Route 66 slipped into rapid decline in the late 1970s, modernism was in the process of fading as the dominant intellectual model for architecture and intellectual thought in Western society. However, the interstate highways were clearly a product of the modern mentality. The interstates were unadorned, disassociated from the past, efficient, and used materials such as reinforced concrete and macadam in a simple "honest" manner. The modern, rational, interstate highway system (conceived in the ultramodernist 1950s) replaced the earlier Route 66, a varied vernacular corridor already rich in the type of cultural and historical references and vernacular whimsy that postmodernists such as Venturi later admired.

Many people living in the postmodern 1980s and 1990s who were accustomed to driving the interstates began to relish the concept of traveling on Route 66, which, in retrospect, appeared appealingly postmodern to them. Although Route 66 preceded the interstates, its complexity and cultural iconography anticipated postmodern sensibilities. Those who remember and praise Route 66 may do so partly because the highway offers unregulated and nonuniform experiences, a play of applied colors and surfaces. In a sense, Route 66 enthusiasts are observers in a postmodern era who are stuck with a modernist transportation system (the interstates) looking back with nostalgia at a quirky highway (Route 66) that better suits their mentality.

Although the historic and cultural significance of Route 66 is mostly a product of cultural forces rather than historical realities, the highway and its predecessors that ran along the same corridor did play a significant role in American history. Route 66 also currently functions as a humanized linear community stretching across a large swath of America where otherwise obscure people have achieved fame and recognition. Often in old age, Route 66 personalities have achieved notoriety at a time in life when people typically relish telling stories of the past. Formerly unknown people, such as the late Lucille Hamon of Oklahoma known as the "Mother of the Mother Road," became Route 66 celebrities because of their association with the famous highway. The operators of decaying tourist courts, souvenir salesmen, hermits, and diner owners are routinely interviewed as American pundits by magazines such as *National Geographic* and *Newsweek* and by European and Japanese television and are featured in books such as Jon Robinson's *Route 66: Lives on the Road*, published in 2001. On historic Route 66, the usual social order becomes reversed when reporters and sometimes wealthy tourists come to visit with and interview 'everyday' people and listen to *their* stories.

On Route 66 in the late 1990s and early 2000s, one could still visit funky vernacular visitor centers operated by eccentrics such as Bob Waldmeir, a bohemian loner whose father invented the corn dog on Route 66 in Illinois, and patronize unique family-owned businesses such as the Pop Hicks Restaurant in Clinton, Oklahoma. Many Route 66 tourists may believe that they are seeing America as it was, but of course this is not entirely true. They are seeing the quiet shadow of travel in America before the interstate highway, a living American ruin. All of the attention and love that Route 66 receives has not prevented the historic highway and its communities from being often neglected and endangered. As more and more tributes, books, magazine articles, and are written about the highway and more and more Web sites are created about it, the motels, gas stations, and cafés along Route 66 as well as the pavement itself continue to be left to deteriorate or be demolished.

CHAPTER FIVE

Saving the Mythic Ruins

Although celebrated in song, in print, and on the Internet, and beloved by thousands, Route 66 is disappearing. Nearly every year more sites are lost: the 66 Park-In Theatre, St. Louis, demolished in 1994; the Coral Courts motel in St. Louis (a property that was listed in the National Register of Historic Places), demolished in 1995; the Club Cafe in Santa Rosa, demolished in 1998 (figure 14); the New Mexico Museum of the Old West, Moriarty, demolished in 2003; Stanley Cour-Tel, St. Louis County, Missouri, demolished in 2003. The list goes on. Other landmarks, such as the El Vado Motel in Albuquerque, have been seriously threatened by development in recent years. Many other sites along the highway, such as adobe gas stations and wooden tourist cabins, are simply being left to deteriorate into ruins that will soon become unrecognizable unless they are restored or at least stabilized. A few key sites have been preserved in recent years—notably, the magnificent Tower Station in Shamrock, Texas (figure 15), and the Blue Swallow Motel in Tucumcari, New Mexico (figure 16), but unfortunately, widespread enthusiasm for Route 66 has not yet translated into widespread preservation.

FIGURE 14. Remains of the famous Club Cafe,
demolished in 1998. Photo by author, October 1998.

Route 66 presents many challenges to those who wish to
safeguard and interpret it for visitors. The most significant of these
is that many historic resources, such as roadside architecture and
bridges along the route, are obsolete and large, and saving them is often
difficult to justify in economic terms. Coordinating preservation
professionals, enthusiasts and members of communities along the

FIGURE 15. Recently restored Tower Station and U-Drop Inn
built in 1936, Shamrock, Texas. Photo by author, March 2006.

historic twenty-four-hundred-mile corridor, which passes through
eight states with diverse histories, climates, and landscapes, intro-
duces another serious preservation problem. In addition, Route 66
possesses strong cultural meanings, making accurate historical interpretation difficult because, as discussed in chapter 4, many people
with an interest in the highway also have entrenched opinions about

the nature of its significance in American history and culture and may become offended at interpretations that don't match their own.

This chapter describes many of the issues and challenges faced by those who are interested in saving and interpreting Route 66. It then discusses current and past efforts to preserve and interpret the highway. Finally, the chapter provides possible strategies to coordinate preservationists and enthusiasts, create accurate, engaging interpretive materials, and develop heritage tourism programs.

The primary reason Route 66 has lost so many landmarks is that the majority of historic motels, cafés, gas stations, and tourist attractions along the route have lost their economic viability, having been bypassed by interstate highways and squeezed out by competition from chain operations. Another factor that endangers old road-related businesses is that they often occupy large lots that make ideal sites for new industrial parks, "big box" retail stores, or chain motels (figure 17). In addition, many historic gas stations have been lost because they occupied prime corner locations, were bought out by large oil companies, or because environmental regulations involving underground fuel storage tanks passed in the 1980s require expensive retrofits and equipment that small operators could not afford.[1] Preserving twentieth-century road-related architecture and structures is a difficult pursuit, and efforts to date on Route 66 have been spotty.

One of the threats to historic Route 66 is the danger to the highway itself. A primary mission of any state department of transportation is to replace aging pavement, bridges and culverts of active roadways with new, safer infrastructure. Without strong historical zoning, increased traffic along old segments of Route 66 may be an impetus for state departments of transportation to widen existing road surfaces and remove aging, narrow bridges, thus destroying characteristics that make the highway historic. While no one can fault the departments of transportation for working to make roads safer, the historic character of the road should be taken into account wherever possible.

In September 1999, the Oklahoma Transportation Commission accepted a bid from a contractor to build a four-lane highway north of Hinton. The project proposed to wipe out about two miles of historic Route 66 pavement. Oklahoma state transportation development spokesman Nico Gomez stated that the old pavement had to be removed because it "didn't meet the existing design standards," and the old segment was replaced.[2] According to Route 66 Corridor

FIGURE 16. Blue Swallow Motel in Tucumcari, New Mexico.
Route 66 landscapes often consist of strips of varied
road-related buildings. Photo by author, October 1998.

Preservation Program coordinator Michael Taylor, "the ultimate challenge in all of this [preserving Route 66] is the state departments of
transportation. In each state the department of transportation is in
the business of making the state's highways safer and usually faster,"
which often compromises the historical integrity of the road.[3]

Taylor cited an example of a recent programmatic agreement between the Arizona State Historic Preservation Office and the state highway department for stretches of historic Route 66 west of Flagstaff. Under this agreement, the highway department was supposed to regulate its own actions in minor repairs to historic segments of road and submit only actions involving more significant repairs to the state historic preservation office for its review and approval. Unfortunately, not long after the agreement was signed, a local Route 66 activist observed the highway department paving over an entire original concrete stretch with asphalt. As it turned out, the parties to the agreement had signed off on the project, violating the spirit of the programmatic agreement. Taylor said that preservationists and Route 66 enthusiasts need to communicate more effectively in order to save historically significant road alignments.[4]

Additional tourism will increase traffic on old sections of Route 66, and without legal protection and professional oversight of historic

FIGURE 17. Many Route 66 landmarks near the larger cities, such as the Bel-Air Drive In near St. Louis, Missouri, have fallen victim to development pressure. Photo by author, September 1998.

resources, the traffic may encourage unsympathetic new development and destruction of not only the highway itself but also historic sites along it. More visitors may create pressure to replace historic buildings and landscapes with new tourist attractions, glitzy diners, and nonhistoric streamlined gas stations designed to mimic historic structures.

To retain their historical significance, properties and landscapes must keep their historical "integrity." Historical integrity means that the significant features, such as prominent porches, original windows, and stylistic ornamentation that make a building unique and recognizable remain. Historical integrity means that if a person from the past were transported to the present, he or she would be able to easily recognize a given historic place. The federal government has developed a set of general standards called the *Secretary of the Interior's Standards for Rehabilitation and Guidelines for Rehabilitating Historic Buildings*, which act as the premier guide in the United States for those seeking to retain the historical integrity of buildings and structures.[5] These standards, which are available from the National Park Service, should be used in any work done to historic Route 66 structures.[6] Of course, the ultimate insult to historical integrity is demolition.

In addition to retaining significant features, historical integrity means not making distracting nonhistoric or speculative additions to historic structures. An example of creating a false historic image on Route 66 would be to remodel a simple roadside café by adding chrome, art deco lighting, and other decorative elements that would make it look like a classic northeastern diner. Few, if any stainless steel, streamlined diners existed along Route 66, and to build them now, without clearly identifying them as of a recent vintage, would falsify the highway's history and degrade the authenticity of the experience of those who tour it.

The Route 66 Diner, a faux historic "diner" created from the remains of a defunct gas station in 1987 on historic Route 66 in Albuquerque, New Mexico, stands as an example of a nonhistoric intrusion that reduces the integrity of that area of Route 66. The diner is located not far from another distracting addition to the Route 66 landscape, the recent reconstruction of the 1902 Alvarado Hotel, which was demolished in the 1970s. This new building, reminiscent of the elegant old hotel designed by Mary Jane Colter, which occupied the same site, adds more interest to downtown Albuquerque, but reduces the historical integrity of the area because it causes confusion between what is new and what is historic. In contrast, the restored "pueblo-deco" Kimo theater farther west on Central Avenue is an Albuquerque landmark that retains a high degree of authenticity and integrity and helps create a meaningful experience of old Route 66 (Figure 18).

Another example of the destructive treatment of a historic building on Route 66 is the remodeling of the historic Union Bus Depot in Lebanon, Missouri. This building was unsympathetically rehabilitated and reused as a furniture store (plate 13 and figure 19).[7] In the process, the building became nearly unrecognizable.

While prudently designed and marketed new businesses can certainly enhance historic Route 66, care must be taken to ensure that people do not confuse these recent additions with historic sites and that historic buildings keep enough historical integrity to be recognizable and interesting. Perhaps a more appropriate reuse for the Lebanon bus station would have been a café called the "Bus Stop,"

FIGURE 18. Kimo Theater, Albuquerque, New Mexico.
Photo by author, August 2003.

FIGURE 19. The Union Bus Depot in Lebanon, Missouri,
has lost the characteristics that make it a recognizable
historic building. Photo by author, September 1988.

located in a rehabilitated but not remodeled building. Not only must
individual buildings be preserved, but the landscapes that surround
them need to be saved as well. Without at least some of its original
rural or urban context, a historic Route 66 motel or roadside trading
post may only be a sad reminder of a lost and dead past. The surrounding context allows visitors and neighbors to appreciate a historic building's original function and worth more fully.

The Secretary of the Interior's Standards for the Treatment of Historic
Properties with Guidelines for the Treatments of Cultural Landscapes
defines a cultural landscape as:

> a geographic area (including both cultural and natural
> resources and the wildlife or domestic animals therein), asso-
> ciated with a historic event, activity, or person or exhibiting
> other cultural or aesthetic values. There are four general types
> of cultural landscapes, not mutually exclusive: historic sites,

historic designed landscapes, historic vernacular landscapes, and ethnographic landscapes.[8]

Essentially, a cultural landscape is a geographic area, which can be a linear corridor, where human activities have left identifiable, related traces on the natural terrain. The entire length of Route 66 makes up a linear cultural landscape in which remnants of the many activities related to traveling by vehicle can be observed and experienced. Highway activities include driving, servicing automobiles and trucks, spending a night, buying fuel, eating meals, buying souvenirs, and visiting natural attractions and cultural sites. The resulting structures, such as the highway, bridges, and culverts and buildings, including service stations, motels, cafés, souvenir shops, and parks, add interest and authenticity to the historic corridor. In addition to automobile and truck-related landscapes, Route 66 encompasses the remnants of other human activities, such as railroading, mining, farming, and settlement by various ethnic groups dating back at least to the Anasazi.

The preservation of vast cultural landscapes is crucial on Route 66. The views that motorists appreciated on Route 66 in the past helped define their experiences of the route. These views, especially in the West, could extend for miles and included not only the immediate roadside but distant mountains and canyons as well. Although natural conservation and historic preservation have been traditionally regarded as separate pursuits, the built and natural environments are never isolated from one another in cultural landscapes. Unfortunately, many preservation agencies, such as state historic preservation offices and local review boards, continue to focus on individual structures and relatively small historic districts, not on cultural landscapes and the preservation of historic and natural resources together, although in recent years a number of preservation professionals have begun adopting a more holistic approach.

An example of the close relationship between history and the natural landscape on Route 66 can be found in the plight of the rocks at Crozier Canyon near Hackberry, Arizona. In the last decade, a stone company has been quarrying the walls of the canyon. A natural formation, the canyon walls functioned as a landmark for motorists who drove old Route 66 through the area.[9]

Route 66 enthusiasts in Arizona oppose the quarrying, even though much of the rock will probably be used in environmentally friendly, water-saving landscaping projects designed to replace chemical and water-consuming lawns throughout arid Arizona. Historian and Route 66 advocate Alfred Runte considers the removal of the rock an "abomination." "There are rocks all over the place," Runte said, "You don't have to use these rocks. This place should have been made a park years ago."[10] The quarrying also played a role in Route 66 enthusiast Bob Waldmire's decision in 1998 to sell his Route 66 visitor center in Hackberry.[11] "I can't handle living between two new rock quarry operations," said Waldmire, son of the inventor of the Cozy Dog, the first corn dog on a stick, developed on Route 66 in Springfield, Illinois, in 1949 at the Cozy Dog Drive-In.[12] Although the quarrying impacts a natural feature, the destruction of the canyon is threatening the historic integrity of the Route 66 cultural landscape in the Hackberry area.

In order for present-day visitors to experience Route 66 in a meaningful way, the landscapes that evolved along Route 66, including natural features and manmade elements from many different eras, need to be preserved as a whole. If too many demolitions take place or too many incompatible additions are made, what remains of old Route 66 will lose its atmosphere and the magic that draws so many tourists from all over the world. This does not mean that Route 66 must become static and be preserved like an artifact in a museum but only that new additions be made in a sensitive, harmonious, manner.

Preservationist David Kammer, a Route 66 advocate who wrote the National Register multiple property nomination for Route 66 in New Mexico, expressed the opinion that Route 66 is a living historical artifact and that new sites, such as the Cadillac Ranch in Amarillo (1974) and the Route 66 Diner in Albuquerque (1987), which came about after Route 66's period of historical significance, have become a valid part of the Route 66 experience for tourists today.[13] This is true for sites that meet two important criteria. The first is that tourists are informed through some type of interpretation or clear architectural cues that the new sites are not historic in the sense of being part of the Route 66 experience before the 1970s. Second, new sites have to be added in a way that does not obliterate or overwhelm the historic character of the road. Add just a few Wal-Mart or Home Depot stores with their massive parking lots and total disregard for the surrounding environment to any given location and the "Route 66 experience" will be lost.

If Route 66 is to be saved, many people with diverse backgrounds will have to be involved and numerous methods and strategies will need to be used. Efforts to preserve historic sites along Route 66 can be divided into two basic categories: the creation of preservation planning tools such as historic resource surveys and the undertaking of concrete projects such as restoring individual road-related buildings and structures.

Historic resource surveys provide systematic identification and documentation of historic resource types that allow preservationists to find and identify the most rare and significant properties and target them for protection and restoration. The Texas Historical Commission, in cooperation with the National Park Service, undertook such an effort in 2002 on the Texas stretch of Route 66. The project included historical research into Route 66 sites and a complete survey of Route 66-related structures in Texas, which resulted in a National Register multiple property nomination for historic Route 66 in Texas.[14] The National Register of Historic Places is a comprehensive list of historic properties nationwide that was developed in 1966.[15] As a property is listed on the National Register, it is researched, photographed and documented.[16] Multiple property nominations identify different but related types of properties, such as "gas stations on Route 66 in Texas" and provide documentation about them and formally establish their historical significance so that it will be easier to list them individually on the National Register later. As of 2006, Illinois, Kansas, Missouri, New Mexico, and Oklahoma have also completed National Register multiple property nominations for their segments of Route 66. And as mentioned in chapter 3, Michael Cassity completed the *Route 66 Corridor National Historic Context Study*, sponsored by the Route 66 Corridor Preservation Program, in 2004. The *Route 66 Corridor National Historic Context Study* was "undertaken to provide a statement of historic context to facilitate the evaluation and the listing of historic resources along historic Route 66 on the National Register of Historic Places."[17] In other words, a context study such as this provides support for anyone who wants to write a National Register of Historic Places nomination for any resource along the entire length of Route 66 by supplying background information and establishing the overall historic value of the highway.

In addition to historic resource surveys and National Register multiple property nominations, an important tool for the protection of the cultural landscapes of Route 66 is listing individual historic sites, districts, and landscapes in the National Register of Historic Places. Listing in the National Register provides formal, federal recognition that a property is historic and assures that the history and historical significance of the property has been researched and documented. This recognition and recordation is particularly important for twentieth-century roadside buildings, such as gas stations, motels, and cafés, because their historical significance has not yet been as widely accepted as has that of earlier sites, such as railroad stations, hotels, and downtown commercial buildings. Fortunately, with each passing year, more and more roadside buildings from the 1950s are reaching the fifty-year threshold. According to National Register guidelines, once a property becomes fifty or more years old it has a better chance of being listed, making its formal recognition as historic site less onerous.

National Register listing offers a property limited protection from federal undertakings under section 106 of the National Historic Preservation Act of 1966.[18] Section 106 regulations define federal undertakings as activities funded in whole or in part by the federal government and those requiring a federal license or permit. Most road projects use a percentage of federal highway money, and even state-funded projects become federal undertakings if they involve work on a bridge that passes over "waters of the United States," which include all navigable waterways and many smaller streams, because such work requires a permit from the U. S. Army Corps of Engineers. Since one of the greatest threats to roadside architecture is road widening, listing sites in the National Register, or at least determining them eligible for listing, will provide a measure of protection.[19]

Section 106 requires that any federal agency or designee funding or permitting an undertaking "take into account" the comments of the state historic preservation office and the federal Advisory Council on Historic Preservation if the council becomes involved. If the state historic preservation office finds that a project will have an "adverse effect," the agency negotiates methods to mitigate the adverse effect with the state historic preservation office and sometimes the Advisory Council. Mitigation measures range from taking photographs of a doomed structure for archival purposes to halting work on the project altogether.

Section 106 often reduces the adverse impact of federal projects on historic properties but rarely stops a project completely. While section 106 can act as a useful tool to force an agency to negotiate, preservationists cannot rely on the law alone to save historic resources. In many instances where a resource stands directly in the path of a project, mitigation ends up being just photographic documentation.[20]

A more stringent law designed to protect historic sites from transportation-related federal undertakings is section 4(f) of the National Transportation Act. This provision requires an agency (usually a state highway department using federal transportation funds) to explore all "feasible and prudent" options to "minimize harm" to a historic property. As with section 106, 4(f) defines a historic property as one listed or eligible for listing in the National Register. While section 106 is essentially advisory, 4(f) directs the Federal Highway Administration and any other federal transportation agency (such as the Federal Aviation Administration) to prepare a meaningful discussion of alternatives for any project that will "take" land from a historic property.[21] In this case, to "take" means that land would actually be condemned or otherwise acquired for direct use by the project.

Another form of "taking" a historic property under section 4(f) is called "constructive use," which means that a project adversely impacts a property to the point that it cannot be used for its historic or intended purpose. An example of constructive use is an elevated highway that passes so close to a historic garden that the highway's shadow would not allow flowers or bushes to grow. Another example is a highway's cutting off access to a historic hotel so that tourists would have no clear way to get to the site. If the Federal Highway Administration determines that a project will harm historic resources, the agency must make all "prudent and feasible" efforts to change the project's design in order to avoid the adverse effect. Legal protections for historic properties can never be taken for granted, however.[22] At this writing, the Bush administration was attempting to weaken section 4(f).[23]

Listing on the National Register has benefits in addition to the possible protections of section 106 and section 4(f). Designation and listing on the National Register make owners of commercial properties eligible for a 20 percent federal tax credit if they rehabilitate their building in a historically sensitive manner using the *Secretary of the Interior's Standards*. In many instances, the tax credit can make the difference between a profitable project and one that does not make money for investors.[24] National Register listing also makes road-related buildings owned by nonprofits, municipalities, and other government entities eligible for enhancement funding under TEA 21 (which replaced a former law called the Intermodal Surface Transportation Efficiency Act, or ISTEA). This program allocates federal highway monies for the rehabilitation of historic structures that are associated with transportation. At least one Route 66 building, the U-Drop Inn in Shamrock, Texas, has been awarded enhancement money.[25]

Another benefit of National Register listing is that it simplifies the creation of local historic districts. Municipalities can pass ordinances that designate any National Register districts within their jurisdiction local historic districts.[26] Municipal governments pass ordinances to create local historic districts in order to protect all historic or "contributing" properties within the district's borders from destructive public or private undertakings. Local historic districts provide much broader protection than National Register districts, because private owners must receive a permit or "certificate of appropriateness" to make significant exterior changes to their building or structure or to its immediate landscape. For this reason, local districts are an important element in protecting historic properties, because National Register listing does not restrict any purely private activities, even the outright demolition of a listed property, by a private owner.

Many historic Route 66 properties, such as the U-Drop Inn in Shamrock, Texas, are listed on the National Register, and cities such as Amarillo, Texas, and Williams, Arizona, have established National Register districts along strips where historic Route 66 passes through town.[27] In addition, several abandoned alignments of old Route 66 that pass through the Kaibab National Forest near Williams, Arizona, have also been listed in the National Register. The Kaibab National Register nomination includes only the original highway right-of-way, including historic pavement (where it exists), bridges, culverts, cuts, and gullies. The listed sections retain their feeling and setting as parts of the historic highway.[28]

As of January 2001, at least sixty-seven individual properties and districts directly associated with Route 66 were listed in the National Register.[29] By 2005, well over a hundred sites and districts on Route 66 had been listed on the National Register, and the National Route 66 Preservation Program planned to list at least fifty more within two years of that date.[30]

A federal initiative to designate Route 66 as the nation's first

National Historic Highway provided another planning tool and resulted in the allocation of some federal funding for preservation work on historic Route 66. The U.S. Congress passed the Route 66 Corridor Act in 1999, which calls for collaboration among Route 66 enthusiasts, state historic preservation offices, and the National Park Service to work toward the designation and safeguarding of the Route 66 corridor. The act defines the Route 66 corridor as "lands owned by the Federal Government and lands owned by State or local government within the immediate vicinity of those portions of the highway formerly designated as United States Route 66, and private land within the immediate vicinity that is owned by persons or entities that are willing to participate in the programs authorized by this Act."[31] This definition assured that private property rights would not be affected, reflecting the political climate in Washington at the time the act was passed.

The Route 66 Corridor Act authorized the National Park Service to perform the following actions: 1) enter into cooperative agreements for planning preservation, rehabilitation, and restoration related to the Route 66 corridor; 2) accept donations of funds, equipment, and supplies; 3) provide federal cost-share grants not to exceed 50 percent of the project cost; 4) provide technical assistance; and 5) coordinate, promote, and stimulate research on the Route 66 corridor. The act cites the *Secretary of the Interior's Standards* as the basis for all authorized rehabilitation work and offers federal assistance for local efforts.[32]

The 1999 Act resulted in the creation of the National Park Service's Route 66 Corridor Preservation Program. This program:

collaborates with private property owners; non-profit organizations; and local, state, federal, and tribal governments to identify, prioritize, and address Route 66 preservation needs. It provides cost-share grants to successful applicants for the preservation and restoration of the most significant and representative properties dating from the route's period of outstanding historical significance, 1926 through 1970. Cost-share grants are also provided for research, planning, oral history, interpretation, and education/outreach projects related to Route 66. The program serves as a clearinghouse of preservation information, and provides limited technical assistance.[33]

One of the most significant contributions of the program has been the Route 66 Preservation Grant and Cost Share Funds program. These matching grants have funded projects such as the repair of the concrete motel units and the neon sign on the office of the Wigwam Motel in Holbrook, Arizona (2003); repairs to the Frontier Motel and Restaurant's neon sign in Truxton, Arizona (2002); and continued funding for the Route 66 Oral History project (2003). Although the federal matching grants for 2003 and 2004 only totaled $134,875 and $121,184 respectively, the grants have provided badly need funds to significant projects.[34]

One of the reasons the total amount of grant money awarded in recent years has been quite limited may be that some owners of historic Route 66 properties find the grant application process confusing and complicated. Bill Kinder, who purchased the historic Blue Swallow Motel in Tucumcari in 2005, said that the requirements of the grant program, such as the need for a structural engineer to approve a task as simple as repaving the driveways, caused too much expense and effort. Kinder also stated that he would need a lawyer to maneuver through the bureaucratic red tape and that the expense didn't justify the amount of any potential grant. He also suggested that rather than giving specific grants to individual property owners, the federal program pay for advertising, such as specifically targeted billboards or ads in the media, for historic motels and other Route 66 businesses to increase their customer base. That way, the businesses themselves could afford to pay for their own maintenance and renovation projects.[35] This may work for sites that are covered by local historical regulations but could encourage destructive alterations to unprotected sites because there would be no oversight of any work done.

A number of preservation projects involving the Route 66 Corridor Preservation Program have been successful on Route 66 in recent years. An example of a particularly innovative project to save a Route 66 historic site is the restoration of the Pig Hip Restaurant in Broadwell, Illinois. Managed by Ernie Edwards, the Pig Hip operated as a café on Route 66 beginning in the 1930s. This project was a joint effort on the part of the National Park Service and the Route 66 Association of Illinois (a private fan group).

In 2003, the Illinois Route 66 Association received a grant from the Route 66 Corridor Preservation Program for about eight thousand dollars to repair the Pig Hip building to prepare it to become a small museum and visitor center. Instead of matching the grant with money, the Illinois association used volunteer labor. The association brought thirty or so local volunteers to the site to participate in "coordinated work days" to rehabilitate the building in compliance with the *Secretary of the Interior's Standards for Rehabilitation*. The program not only saved a significant Illinois Route 66 landmark, but it also trained volunteers in sensitive, hands-on preservation as they worked together with preservation professionals toward a common goal.[36] According to David Gaines, chief of the National Park Service Branch of Long Distance Trails, "Cooperative partnerships [such as the Pig Hip project] offer the greatest potential for effectively dealing with the myriad complexities of managing the diverse resources of Route 66."[37] Route 66 is a perfect venue for the combination of preservation professionalism and the grassroots enthusiasm demonstrated by the Pig Hip project to flourish in.

Adaptive use of Route 66's associated structures often involves converting historic gas stations or cafés into visitor centers, such as the Pig Hip and the Tower Station and U-Drop Inn building, a 1936 architectural landmark, recently restored as a visitor and community center.[38] Turning historic road-related buildings into visitor centers is an excellent way in which to reuse them. However, the need for visitor centers is limited, and alternative uses for the hundreds of historic sites on Route 66 need to be found. An interesting adaptive use of a Route 66 structure is the rehabilitation of the abandoned 1929 Chain of Rocks Bridge across the Mississippi River into a pedestrian trail and bikeway, which opened in 1999.[39] Another instructive example of reuse is the Will Rogers Hotel, a historic multistory hotel on Route 66 in Claremore, Oklahoma, rehabilitated in 1997 as affordable housing for the elderly by the Rogers County Historical Society using donations and grants.[40] In addition, many commercial structures along Claremore's Main Street have been converted into antique stores, creating an extensive antique shopping district.[41] Amarillo, Texas, has also converted its Route 66 historic district into a shopping area, which includes restaurants, motels, and other amenities, for antiques and specialty items.

Many towns in regions such as central New Mexico and eastern Arizona, rural Missouri and eastern Oklahoma are in dire need of economic revitalization. The fact that a famous road links these communities may be their best and perhaps only chance to tap into the tourist industry. Route 66 brings tourists to remote communities that they would probably never visit otherwise.

Innovative reuse possibilities exist, such as converting historic tourist courts into small hotels. An example is the San José Motel on South Congress Avenue in Austin, Texas. Although the San José is not on Route 66, the motel serves as a possible model for similar establishments on 66. The San José is an old tourist court recently converted into an upscale motel-hotel. The San José model may work in large and more affluent Route 66 communities such as Flagstaff, Arizona, and Albuquerque, New Mexico. Other uses for defunct historic motels include transforming them into affordable housing, small commercial malls, and even flea markets.[42]

Not all historic motels, hotels, and cafés on Route 66 need to be refitted for some other purpose. Many continue to be used for their original purpose. Some, such as the El Rancho Hotel in Gallup, New Mexico, have been in constant use since construction. Others, like the Aztec Motel built on Route 66 in Albuquerque in 1931, have been reopened after having ceased operation. Before 1991, the Aztec had fallen into disrepair and was "inhabited by prostitutes and drug dealers." In that same year, Mohammed Natha bought the motel, cleaned it up, created strict rules of conduct for residents and guests, and currently operates the facility, offering moderately priced units for tourist accommodation and temporary housing for locals that is safe, clean, and adds to Albuquerque's tax base.[43] Motels such as the Aztec have been maintained and modified over the years, but have never needed a major rehabilitation. The Ariston Café in Litchfield, Illinois, which opened in 1924, stands as an example of a historic restaurant on Route 66 that is still intact and in operation. Other examples of Route 66 business still functioning in 2006 include the Wigwam Motel in Holbrook, Arizona, Roy's Café & Motel in Amboy, California, and the Historic Route 66 (formerly Hull's) Motel in Williams, Arizona. Continued occupation of historic structures by local businesses is always the best preservation option so long as the business owners treat the property in a historically sensitive manner.

Some buildings on Route 66 may not be able to be kept in use. Many old roadside structures are already ruins that are either too deteriorated to rehabilitate or are in such remote locations that there's no feasible reuse option or both (figure 20). Still, so long as these ruins are not vandalized and efforts are made to stabilize them, they could last for generations, especially in arid regions. While the majority of historic Route 66 resources should be actively preserved, there is no need to make every motel functional again or to turn every old gas station into a visitor center. In fact, to do so would destroy the vacant, eerie quality that many visitors to Route 66 enjoy.

Preserving historic sites and cultural landscapes is only one aspect of saving Route 66. In order for the historic corridor to remain viable, it must attract tourists to help pay for preservation efforts and to help generate enthusiasm for the highway on the local level. And in order for tourists to understand and appreciate Route 66, they must have access to interpretive materials, such as guidebooks, roadside signs, visitor's centers and museums, and historical narratives. Efforts to further develop Route 66 as a tour route should include a broad effort to integrate layers of historic events into an inclusive, historically accurate, exciting, and comprehensive story. To achieve this, public historians should interpret the history of Route 66 from a broad variety of sources.

Many of the individuals who currently operate visitor centers and museums along Route 66 can remember the road and interpret its history firsthand. However, the majority of these people will retire within the next few years, making it necessary for a new generation of historians and preservationists to step in and develop methods of interpreting Route 66 without the benefit of direct memory.

Methods of interpretation include Route 66 museums, directional signs, wayside exhibits, guide books, guided tours, pamphlets about individual sites, annotated maps, and media presentations such as films, CDs, tapes, and AM radio broadcasts to passing vehicles. Although interpretive materials should be the product of extensive historical research aided by eyewitness accounts of Americans who have used and continue to use the corridor, unsubstantiated myths about Route 66 may be communicated, so long as myths are clearly identified as such and not confused with history. Interpretation should relate what travelers on Route 66 actually experienced and not merely repeat the clichés often expressed by nostalgic enthusiasts. Michael Taylor sees "One of the roles of the Park Service as providing interpretation (for those interested in Route 66) that is as factual as possible, in part, by using existing National Register historic contexts for the highway and creating additional contexts, if needed." Taylor cited one sensitive area of Route 66 history as the "bigotry and racism"

FIGURE 20. Route 66 ruin in New Mexico. Many
contemporary tourists travel Route 66 to experience its eerie,
vacant quality. Photo by author, October 1998.

that existed in America during the historic Route 66 era and certainly
existed on the road itself. "The Park Service is in a position to bring
out the 'good, bad, and the ugly' of Route 66," he said.[44]

Interpretative materials should discuss Route 66 in its historical
contexts. As historians relate the story of Route 66, they should keep in
mind that most early autoroutes, including Route 66, encompass layers of transportation and regional history through different periods. As
discussed earlier, most sections of Route 66 parallel nineteenth-century
wagon roads, which themselves often followed trails blazed earlier by
Native Americans. In addition, any interpretation of Route 66 should
include information about the railroad era when most Route 66 towns
formed and about the cultural stereotypes of Native Americans and
Mexican Americans that the railroads promoted, which would provide
a background for the cultural and ethnographic imagery associated
with southwestern cultures later used on Route 66.

In order to channel tourism so that visitation helps safeguard the route rather than hurting it, communities need to develop comprehensive preservation plans that include tools such as the establishment of National Register districts, scenic easements, and local historic districts.

Scenic America, a private, nonprofit organization dedicated to preserving American cultural landscapes, recommends developing preservation management plans that use a combination of tools to protect historic "scenic byways." The organization defines scenic byways as "secondary roads having significant cultural, historic, scenic, geological or natural features." Scenic byways often include vistas, rest areas, and interpretive sites. Thirty-four state governments have designated over thirty-five thousand miles of scenic highways throughout the United States.[45] Certainly, the longer intact segments of Route 66 would qualify, such as the 130-mile segment in Arizona that deviates from Interstate 40 and passes through Seligman, which has been designated as a state scenic route.[46]

In addition to a management plan, Scenic America recommends five measures for protecting scenic byways. The first recommendation is to establish a program to protect significant trees and plantings from being routinely removed by highway maintenance crews of the state highway department and other entities. The second measure would limit outdoor advertising.[47] The third recommendation is to create a framework for scenic easements and a process by which landowners could sell or donate scenic easements to state governments or private nonprofit organizations to protect landscapes. The fourth measure would encourage strong local participation and coordination with relevant governmental agencies, and the fifth would develop special operations and maintenance standards for the highway. These special standards would cover activities such as road widening, straightening, guardrail alterations, and changes in road grade that may threaten the characteristics of the highway that make it historic and scenic.[48] Highway enthusiasts and local governments should work with state departments of transportation and state historic preservation offices to develop special safety and maintenance guidelines for historic segments of Route 66.

Route 66 should be the link and justification for a plethora of local efforts to preserve the corridor guided and supported by the state historic preservation offices, the National Park Service, and of course, the Route 66 Corridor Preservation Program, at least until 2009, when the program is set to expire. Many towns along Route 66 could adopt the National Trust for Historic Preservation's Main Street Program to assist local business owners in economic revitalization and historic preservation of commercial buildings.[49] When the National Park Service Route 66 Corridor Preservation Program expires, private preservation organizations and enthusiast groups will have to form the nucleus of future collaborations among communities, historians, and government.

Another goal of historic road designation is to strengthen regional and local identities. Interest in Route 66 can bring, and already has brought, many communities together because they share a history as well as a physical transportation link. Revitalizing Route 66 spurs community pride and historical awareness in little-known places such as Rolla, Missouri; Galena, Kansas; and Vega, Texas, helping both residents and tourists find new value and take new pride in these communities. Learning the transportation history of their town may help residents understand its links to the broader currents of American history and hopefully inspire further preservation efforts. When locals observe people from other states and even foreign countries stopping in their town to visit and photograph an old motel or gas station, they are likely to take notice and become curious as to why outsiders are interested and perhaps come to take pride in the fact that others are interested in the historic resources of their municipality. Additional tourism on Route 66 may also encourage people to visit sites and communities that are within a convenient drive of the highway but not directly on the road, such as Palo Duro Canyon, Texas, and Santa Fe, New Mexico (although Santa Fe was on historic Route 66 from 1927 to 1937).

Historic roads such as Route 66 have an inherent advantage over thematic "heritage areas," such as artificial heritage routes developed in many states. Examples include Pennsylvania's "Industrial Heritage Route" (the Path of Progress) and the "Civil War Heritage Trail" in Tennessee. Old roads are historic in *themselves* and act naturally as a powerful and authentic unifying theme that carries tourists along. The phrase "get your kicks on Route 66" has more appeal than "drive the Path of Progress" (or any other invented heritage route) could ever obtain. Creating well-publicized and clearly marked tour routes along traditional transportation routes is an effective way to interpret historic resources and their contexts. Tour routes increase public appreciation and heighten concern for historic structures and sites, as long as historic preservation regulations are in effect to protect historic structures and landscapes from incompatible development.

Designating historic Route 66 as a tour route and protecting its views, vernacular roadside architecture, and original alignments would be to utilize the automobile and its history as an agent of environmental preservation rather than a harbinger of environmental degradation. Adaptive use and interpretation of Route 66 should include multiuse, nonmotorized trails along little-used or abandoned segments of historic highway and self-guided auto tour routes along stretches of active historic highway.

Although cultural tourism can have negative impacts on historic resources, effective preservation would be difficult without visitors to enjoy the sites. Public interest in Route 66 is what drives preservation efforts, and some of that interest arises because merchants in Route 66 communities view the road as a potential source of revenue from tourists. Without an economic incentive, many property owners might view historical regulations as merely an annoyance and choose to circumvent the law in order to make a return on their property. At present, there are little data to indicate what economic impact historic Route 66 has on local economies.[50] Tabulating such economic data would be useful as a tool to promote preservation efforts.

Reusing historic Route 66 allows today's travelers to rediscover the remote American landscapes that many of their parents and grandparents discovered on their auto vacations. A comprehensive tour route over historic pathways can provide an authentic alternative to artificial environments such as Disney World in Florida or even the controlled experience of historic Colonial Williamsburg, Virginia. The communities along Route 66 are living, changing places where layers of history, from prehistoric Indian times to the present, can be seen and enjoyed.

The effective preservation of historic resources requires, three things: first, people must discover and appreciate their community's history and the significance of its structures and landscapes; second, people in a city, town, or county must work together to save and rehabilitate structures, and third, municipalities must enact local historic zoning ordinances to prevent those who do not appreciate history and a livable environment from destroying significant buildings, structures, and landscapes. Ultimately, the key to historic preservation lies not with the National Park Service and other federal or state agencies but within the communities themselves.

Route 66 was the first long-distance U.S. highway officially identified and funded by the federal government as a historic highway. Because Route 66 has the widest public support and the largest pool of enthusiasts of any American highway, the preservation of Route 66 will have a significant influence on efforts to save other historic American highways.

Summary and Conclusion

Even though it was not the longest, or the first, American highway, Route 66 is the most famous road in the United States and possibly the world. Part of the reason Route 66 gained such a distinct identity in popular culture is that the western half of this historic highway ran through the tourist destinations of New Mexico and Arizona on its way to southern California.

When Route 66 opened in 1926, the Southwest was already a focus of tourism. In the late nineteenth and early twentieth centuries, railroads such as the Santa Fe and the Union Pacific created popular myths about the region to increase ridership on their lines and fill their western railroad hotels with eastern tourists. After 1900, the Fred Harvey Company built a string of regionally themed hotels, including the Alvarado in Albuquerque (1902) and the El Tovar (1905) beside the Grand Canyon. Fred Harvey's main architect, Mary Jane Colter, borrowed heavily from pueblo and Spanish colonial architecture. She consciously created "fiction in three dimensions" by purposely making her buildings look timeworn. Both the Santa Fe train tracks and Fred Harvey architecture closely paralleled the route that would become Route 66.

The railroads produced brochures full of pictures of Indians in native dress, printed colorful calendars with southwestern themes, took out full-page ads in major periodicals depicting exotic scenes featuring Pueblo Indians, and even gave their trains names such as the "Navajo," the "Chief," and the "Super Chief." These efforts helped to transform "wild" Indians into tamed curiosities, cowpunchers into "wholesome" Anglo Saxon heroes, Pueblo cultures into "lost" civilizations, and Mexican Americans into "colorful" señoritas and dons in the minds of many Anglo tourists. A few decades of intensive marketing transformed what had previously been perceived as a barren wasteland into a "land of enchantment."

In the 1930s, the automobile overtook the passenger train as the primary mode of long-distance passenger travel. As train ridership decreased, traffic on Route 66 increased. To entice tourists to take Route 66, businesspeople in Route 66 communities and the U.S. Route 66 Highway Association (formed in 1927 by Cyrus Avery to promote the new highway) used the already established stereotypical ideas about Native American culture, Mexican Americans, and the cowboy to create roadside environments designed to entice auto tourists to stop. When movies emerged in the twentieth century, the popular genre of the western film added to the lore of the Southwest and Route 66, which took tourists westward through many of the locations where the movies were set and filmed right through to Hollywood itself. Many Hollywood celebrities, such as Ronald Reagan and Jackie Cooper, stayed at the El Rancho Hotel in Gallup, New Mexico, on Route 66, while filming in the 1950s and 1960s. A slew of western movies were filmed in the Gallup area from the 1940s through the 1960s.[1]

After Route 66 became the primary auto and truck route through the Southwest, the highway began to become well known in its own right. In the late 1930s and 1940s, the legend of the "Okies" was added to the lore of Route 66, a legend that, in part, grew out of John Steinbeck's *The Grapes of Wrath*, published in 1939. Bobby Troup's 1946 song "Route 66" and the collective experiences of millions of postwar tourists, made the name "Route 66" popular enough to become the title of a television show in the 1960s, a time when interstate highways had already begun to replace the old road.

After the highway officially ceased to exist in 1985, a grassroots movement formed to save the memory of a highway that had become too famous to be forgotten. Route 66 became an object of nostalgia fueled by the highway's associations with Indians, Mexicans, cowboys, the Okies, deserts, and family vacations. The highway also became the focus of a general glorification of 1950s American automobile culture. Route 66 came to represent a host of alluring American concepts such as the Wild West, individualism, innocence, self-realization, patriotism, coming-of-age, and the freedom of the open road. The Route 66 shield has become a popular icon that represents these ideas and America itself. With its complexity, multiple meanings, kitsch, and alluring cultural iconography, historic Route 66 appealed to the postmodern mentality of the 1980s, 1990s, and beyond.

In essence, the fame of Route 66 resulted from marketing efforts, first by the railroads and then by Route 66 businesses, communities along the highway, and the U.S 66 Highway Association. Currently, many businesses along historic Route 66 and regional historic Route 66 fan groups, such as the Arizona Route 66 Association, continue to promote the highway through Route 66-themed advertisements, events, and products. Route 66 is very much a consequence of the evolution of American capitalism and its marketing techniques from the late nineteenth century to the present and continues to inspire new modes of popularity as our society evolves.

Despite all of the marketing and hype, the highway continues to function as a genuine linear community from Chicago to Los Angeles. Whenever one gets on Route 66, whether on a part of it that crosses an Illinois prairie or an Arizona desert, one finds a distinct atmosphere of friendliness. It is very difficult not to engage in pleasant conversations on Route 66. While this may or may have not have been consistently true ever since the road was built, the congeniality of people on Route 66 today provides a welcome relief from the standardized and often alienating social environments of business located on interstate exchanges.

Despite its official demise, Route 66 continues to lead travelers through the fascinating landscapes of the prairies of the Midwest, the piney forests of the Upper South, the vast expanses of the Great Plains, and the deserts and mountains of the Southwest all the way to the Santa Monica Pier. A contemporary Web site dedicated to Route 66 in Texas reads: "Route 66 the highway became the romance of the west and Texas was the gateway to this great adventure. Cowboys and Indians, trains and Disneyland, outlaws and movie stars mingled together on this highway of legend that ended at the vast reaches of the Pacific Ocean."[2] If preserved and protected, Route 66 will function as a dynamic historic spectacle for generations to come.

Notes

Introduction

1. Interview with Route 66 merchant in Arizona, October 4, 1998.
2. Leah Dilworth, "Tourists and Indians in Fred Harvey's Southwest," in *Seeing & Being Seen: Tourism in the American West*, ed. David M. Wrobel and Patrick T. Long, 142–64 (Lawrence: University Press of Kansas, 2001).
3. Michael Taylor, director of Route 66 Corridor Preservation Program, in discussion with the author, August 2003.
4. Santa Fe Inn advertisement, "Where Shall We Stay," *National Geographic*, February 1938, supplemental.
5. Thomas Arthur Repp, *Route 66: The Empires of Amusement* (Lynwood, WA: Mock Turtle Press, 1999), 1–5.
6. Tom Teague, Bob Waldmire, and Lon Haldeman, *Searching for Route 66*, 2nd ed. (Springfield, IL: Samizdat House, 1996), 1.
7. Michael Taylor, director of Route 66 Corridor Preservation Program, in discussion with the author, August 2003. According to Taylor, no hard data exists on how much money Route 66 communities are actually receiving from tourism related to historic Route 66.
8. Interview with Route 66 visitor center volunteer, Oklahoma, September 28, 1998. *Great Drives: A Cross-Country Trek from Chicago, Illinois, to Santa Monica, California*, directed by Robert Townsend, Public Broadcasting System, 1996. David Lamb, "Route 66: Romancing the Road," *National Geographic*, September 1997, 47–64. Malcolm Jones, Jr., "The Highway That's the Best." *Newsweek*, November 16, 1992, 92–95.

9. Interview with German tourists, Seligman, AZ, October 4, 1998.

10. Interview with Illinois Route 66 merchant, September 24, 1998.

11. Interview with Illinois gas station operator, September 26, 1998.

12. Michael Taylor, director of Route 66 Corridor Preservation Program, in discussion with the author, August 2003.

13. Michael Wallis, "Route 66, the Mother Road" (lecture, Route 66 Expo, Shamrock, TX, October 2, 1998).

Chapter One

1. Leah Dilworth, "Tourists and Indians in Fred Harvey's Southwest," in *Seeing and Being Seen: Tourism in the American West,* ed. David M. Wrobel and Patrick T. Long (Lawrence: University Press of Kansas, 2001), 145.

2. Alfred Runte, "Promoting the Golden West: Advertising and the Railroad," *California History,* Spring 1991, 63.

3. Thomas Pew Jr., "Route 66, a Ghost Road" *American Heritage,* July 1977, 26.

4. Leon C. Metz, *Roadside History of Texas* (Missoula, MT: Mountain Press Publishing, 1994), 390.

5. Pew Jr., "Route 66," 26.

6. U.S. Department of the Interior, National Park Service, *Special Resource Study: Route 66* (Denver: U.S. Department of the Interior, 1995), 5.

7. Pew Jr., "Route 66," 26.

8. Claire Shepherd-Lanier, "Trading on Tradition: Mary Jane Colter and the Romantic Appeal of Harvey House Architecture," *Journal of the Southwest,* Summer 1996, 163.

9. Bob Moore and Patrick Grauwels, *Route 66: The Illustrated Guidebook to the Mother Road* (Williams, AZ: Roadbook International, 1998), 33, 87, and 76.

10. New Mexico State Highway Department, "New Mexico Official Road Map" (Santa Fe: New Mexico State Highway Department, 1954). "The Land of Enchantment" is the state of New Mexico's slogan. According to the New Mexico blue book "the New Mexico nickname was first noted in the title of a book by Lillian Whiting in 1906. In 1935, the state tourism director designed a brochure using the tag line of 'The Land of Enchantment.' That same year, 'New Mexico Magazine' started advertising using the slogan." According to Melissa Papke and Cynthia Kirkeby of ClassBrain, Inc. (found at classbrain.com) "New Mexico started using 'The Land of Enchantment' slogan after the state of Florida stole their original slogan of 'The Sunshine State.' Because of this fact, New Mexico had their new slogan copyrighted" (http://www.classbrain.com/artaskcb/publish/article_107.shtml [accessed October 1, 2006]).

11. Chris Wilson, *The Myth of Santa Fe: Creating a Modern Regional Tradition* (Albuquerque: University of New Mexico Press, 1997), 48–52.

12. Duncan Heath and Judy Boreham, *Introducing Romanticism* (Cambridge: Icon Books, 2000).

13. Hoxie Neale Fairchild, *The Noble Savage: A Study in Romantic Naturalism* (New York: Russell and Russell, 1961), 15–20.

14. The romantic philosopher Jean Jacques Rousseau coined the term "noble savage."

15. Julie Scimmel, "Inventing the Indian," in *The West as America: Reinterpreting Images of the Frontier*, ed. William H. Truettner (Washington, D.C.: Smithsonian Institution Press, 1991), 149–89.

16. Scimmel, "Inventing the Indian," 151.

17. Patricia Nelson Limerick, *The Legacy of Conquest: The Unbroken Past of the American West* (New York: W. W. Norton, 1987), 123.

18. George Catlin, *North American Indians: Being Letters and Notes on Their Manners, Customs, and Conditions, Written During Eight Years' Travel Amongst the Wildest Tribes in North America, 1832–1839*, 2 vols. (London: George Catlin, 1880), 1:293.

19. Limerick, *The Legacy of Conquest*, 185.

20. Steven Roach, "Classicizing America's Indian in the Mid-Nineteenth Century: James Longacre's Indian Cent" (history of art honors thesis, University of Michigan, 2002), http://www.michigancoinclub.org/classicizing.htm (accessed April 18, 2006).

21. Renato Rosaldo, *Culture and Truth: The Remaking of Social Analysis* (Boston: Beacon Press, 1993), vii. Rosaldo is a professor of cultural and social anthropology at Stanford University and former director of the Stanford University Center for Chicano Research. A reference to "imperialist nostalgia" in rail tourism to the Southwest can be found in Leah Dilworth's "Tourists and Indians in Fred Harvey's Southwest," 145.

22. Cited in Lloyd E. Hudman, "Tourism and the West," *Journal of the West*, July 1994, 68.

23. Edwin L. Wade, "The Ethnic Market in the Southwest 1880–1980," in *Objects and Others: Essays on Museums and Material Culture*, ed. George W. Stocking Jr., History of Anthropology Series 3 (Madison: University of Wisconsin Press, 1985), 169.

24. Billy M. Jones, *Health Seekers in the Southwest: 1817–1900* (Norman: University of Oklahoma Press, 1967), 88–95.

25. Marta Weigle and Peter White, *The Lore of New Mexico* (Albuquerque: University of New Mexico Press, 1988), 22.

26. Runte, "Promoting the Golden West," 63.

27. Weigle and White, *The Lore of New Mexico*, 53.

28. Runte, "Promoting the Golden West," 63.

29. Hudman, "Tourism and the West," 69.

30. Weigle and White, *The Lore of New Mexico*, 57. A depiction of Indian art appeared in a 1903 AT&SF advertisement for the "California Limited," and a line drawing of an Indian woman appeared in an advertisement in the December 1906 edition of *Harper's Magazine*.

31. Gilbert H. Grosvenor, "The Land of the Best," *National Geographic*, April 24, 1916, 328.

32. N. H. Darton, "The Southwest, Its Splendid Natural Resources, Agricultural Wealth, and Scenic Beauty," *National Geographic*, August 21, 1910, 643–44.

33. Runte, "Promoting the Golden West," 65.

34. Hal Rothman, *Preserving Different Pasts: The American National Monuments* (Urbana: University of Illinois Press, 1989), 58.

35. Kerwin L. Klein, "Frontier Products: Tourism, Consumerism, and the Southwestern Public Lands, 1890–1990," *Pacific Historical Review* 62 (February 1993): 45.

36. Rothman, *Preserving Different Pasts*, 63.

37. Runte, "Promoting the Golden West," 63.

38. Wilson, *Myth of Santa Fe*, 91.

39. "Atchison, Topeka, & Santa Fe Railroad," *Harper's Magazine*, December 1903, November 1910, and June, 1912 and "Southern Pacific Railroad," *Harper's Magazine*, June 1907.

40. Santa Fe Railroad advertisements in *Harper's Magazine* in June 1921 and November 1926. The 1926 promotion for the "Chief" utilizes the Indian warrior in feathered headdress image so often used by subsequent Route 66 roadside businesses.

41. Wilson, *Myth of Santa Fe*, 90.

42. Leah Dilworth, *Imagining Indians in the Southwest: Persistent Visions of a Primitive Past* (Washington, D.C.: Smithsonian Institution Press, 1996), 85.

43. Edwin L. Wade, "The Ethnic Market in the Southwest," 169.

44. F. Douglas, *Denver Art Museum* leaflet 30 (August 1931) cited in Edwin Wade, "The Ethnic Art Market in the Southwest, 1880–1980," 44.

45. Weigle and White, *Lore of New Mexico*, 64.

46. Weigle and White, *Lore of New Mexico*, 49.

47. Wilson, *Myth of Santa Fe*, 90.

48. Dilworth, *Imagining Indians*, 81.

49. Hudman, "Tourism and the West," 69.

50. Claire Shepherd-Lanier, "Trading on Tradition," 165.

51. Arnold Berke, "Drawing from the Desert, Architect Mary Colter Told Stories in Stone," *Preservation*, July/August 1997, 42.

52. Berke, "Drawing from the Desert," 39.

53. Marta Weigle, "Southwest Lures: Innocents Detoured, Incensed Determined," *Journal of the Southwest*, Winter 1990, 526.

54. New Mexico History Index, "Charles Lummis," http://www.cia-g.com/~rockets/dNMhist.lummis (accessed July 18, 2002).

55. Abigail A. Van Slyck, "Racial Stereotypes and the Southwest's Vernacular Architecture," in *Gender, Class, and Shelter*, Perspectives in Vernacular Architecture 5, ed. Elizabeth C. Crowley and Carter L. Hudgins (Knoxville: University of Tennessee Press, 1995), 60.

56. Limerick, *Legacy of Conquest*, 240.

57. Weigle, "Southwest Lures," 528.

58. Charles F. Lummis, *The Land of Poco Tiempo* (1893; repr., New York: Charles Scribner's Sons, 1913), 3.

59. Van Slyck, "Racial Stereotypes and the Southwest," 97.

60. Dilworth, *Imagining Indians*, 101.

61. William W. Savage Jr., *Cowboy Life: Reconstructing an American Myth* (Norman: University of Oklahoma Press, 1975), 7.

62. Savage, *Cowboy Life*, 8.

63. Kevin S. Blake, "Zane Grey and Images of the American West," *Geographic Review*, April 1995, 202–13.

64. Public Broadcasting System, "New Perspectives on the West," http://www.pbs.org/weta/thewest/people/s_z/turner.htm (accessed October 1, 2006).

65. Ben Yagoda, *Will Rogers: A Biography* (New York: Alfred A. Knopf, 1993), 96.

66. Richard Slotkin, *Gunfighter Nation: The Myth of the Frontier in the Twentieth-Century America* (New York: Harper Perennial, 1992), 29–39.

67. M. T. Marsden, "The Popular Western Novel as a Cultural Artifact," *Arizona and the West*, Spring 1978, 207.

68. John Lukacs, "From Camelot to Abilene," *American Heritage*, February 1981, 55.

69. Owen Wister, quoted in John Lukacs, "From Camelot to Abilene," 56.

70. Owen Wister, quoted in John Lukacs, "From Camelot to Abilene," 57.

71. Kenneth W. Porter, "African Americans in the Cattle Industry, 1860s–1880s," in *Peoples of Color in the American West*, ed. Sucheng Chan, Douglas Daniels, Mario T. Garcia, and Terry P. Wilson (Toronto: Heath and Company, 1994), 159.

72. Peggy Robbins, "Will Rogers: The Immortal Cherokee Kid," *American History Illustrated*, July 1974, 6.

73. Reba Neighbors Collins, "Just Plain Will," *The Quill*, May 1990, 44–47.

74. Yagoda, *Will Rogers*, 174.

75. Shepherd-Lanier, "Trading on Tradition," 190.

76. Alan Gowans, *Styles and Types of North American Architecture: Social Function and Cultural Expression* (New York: Harper Collins, 1992), 452.

77. Vintage postcard, ca. 1940, in author's collection. Other examples of tourist-related architecture on Route 66 in the Pueblo revival style include the Zia Lodge, the Zuni Lodge, the Canyon Lodge, the El Jardon Lodge, and the El Vado Court, all in Albuquerque, New Mexico. Route 66 motels in the Spanish Colonial revival style include the chain of Park Plaza motels with locations on Route 66 in St. Louis, Missouri, Tulsa, Oklahoma, Amarillo, Texas, and Flagstaff, Arizona; the Mayflower Motel in Albuquerque, New Mexico; the Tulsa Motel in Tulsa, Oklahoma; and the Mayo Motel in Los Angeles, California. Source, historic postcards, author's collection.

Chapter Two

1. Mark H. Rose, *Interstate, Express Highway Politics, 1941–1956* (Lawrence: The Regents Press of Kansas, 1979), 2.

2. Robert S. Lynd and Helen Merrell Lynd, *Middletown: A Study in American Culture* (San Diego: Harcourt Brace and Company, 1929), 261.

3. Bureau of Labor Statistics, "Consumer Price Index CPI Inflation Calculator," http://146.142.4.24/cgi-bin/cpicalc.pl (accessed June 1, 2006). This site allows anyone to calculate any dollar amount to find its relative value in any year between 1913 and the present. The exact amount the calculator gave was $13,229.80 2006 dollars for $650 1913 dollars.

4. Dorothy R. L. Seratt and Terri Ryburn-Lamont, *Historic and Architectural Resources of Route 66 through Illinois*, National Register of Historic Places

Multiple Property Documentation Form (Washington, D.C.: National Park Service, 1997).

5. The Lincoln Highway Association, *The Lincoln Highway: The Story of a Crusade That Made Transportation History* (New York: Dodd, Mead and Company, 1935), 7.

6. Warren James Belasco "Commercialized Nostalgia: The Origins of the Roadside Strip," in *The Automobile and American Culture*, ed. David L. Lewis and Laurence Goldstein (Ann Arbor: University of Michigan Press, 1983), 107.

7. John A. Jakle, *The Tourist: Travel in Twentieth-Century North America* (Lincoln: University of Nebraska Press, 1985), 154.

8. Walt Whitman, *Leaves of Grass*, http://www.princeton.edu/~batke/logr/log_082.html. The first two stanzas of the poem:
   AFOOT and light-hearted I take to the open road,
   Healthy, free, the world before me,
   The long brown path before me leading wherever I choose.
   Henceforth I ask not good-fortune, I myself am good-fortune,
   Henceforth I whimper no more, postpone no more, need nothing,
   Done with indoor complaints, libraries, querulous criticisms,
   Strong and content I travel the open road.

9. Thomas R. Vale and Geraldine R. Vale, *U.S. 40 Today: Thirty Years of Landscape Change in America* (Madison: University of Wisconsin Press, 1983), 4.

10. Joe McCarthy, "The Lincoln Highway," *American Heritage*, June 1974, 32–38.

11. Lincoln Highway Association, *The Lincoln Highway: The Story of a Crusade that Made Transportation History* (New York: Dodd, Mead and Company, 1935), 2.

12. Carroll Van West et al., *Tennessee Encyclopedia of History and Culture* (Nashville: Tennessee Historical Society, 1998).

13. George Stewart, *U.S. 40: A Cross Section of the United States of America* (Boston: Houghton Mifflin Company, 1953), 5.

14. Lincoln Highway Association, *The Lincoln Highway*, 4.

15. David J. Kammer, *Historic and Architectural Resources of Route 66 through New Mexico Auto Tourism across New Mexico, 1926–1956*, National Register of Historic Places Multiple Property Documentation Form (Washington, D.C.: National Park Service, 1993), 32.

16. Seratt and Ryburn-Lamont, *Historic and Architectural Resources of Route 66*, 12.

17. Although the Meridian Highway was short-lived, the concept turned out to be well ahead of its time. In 2001, the Federal Highway Administration developed plans to extend Interstate 69, to make it a "North American Free Trade Agreement (NAFTA) highway," along a similar route to the east of the Meridian route. This highway, parts of which are now open, will allow trucks to transport goods to and from Canada and Mexico on a direct interstate.

18. Kammer, *Historic and Architectural Resources of Route 66*, 25.

19. Kammer, *Historic and Architectural Resources of Route 66*, 14.

20. Chester H. Liebs, *Main Street to Miracle Mile: American Roadside Architecture* (Boston: Bulfinch Press, 1985), 8.

21. Kammer, *Historic and Architectural Resources of Route 66*, 45.

22. Kammer, *Historic and Architectural Resources of Route 66*, 50.

23. Joseph Interrante, "The Road to Autopia," in *The Automobile and American Culture*, ed. David L. Lewis and Lawrence Goldstein (Ann Arbor: University of Michigan Press, 1983), 94–95.

24. Stewart, *U.S. 40: A Cross Section*, 12.

25. Michael Wallis, *Route 66: The Mother Road* (New York: St. Martin's Press, 1990), 7.

26. Seratt and Ryburn-Lamont, *Historic and Architectural Resources of Route 66*, 13.

27. Wallis, *Route 66: The Mother Road*, 7.

28. William Kaszynski, *Route 66: Images of America's Main Street* (Jefferson, NC: McFarland and Company, Inc., Publishers, 2003), 3.

29. Wallis, *Route 66: The Mother Road*, 8.

30. Kammer, *Historic and Architectural Resources of Route 66*, 9.

31. Michael Wallis, "Route 66, the Mother Road" (lecture, Route 66 Expo, Shamrock, TX, October 2, 1998).

32. Susan Croce Kelly and Quinta Scott, *Route 66: The Highway and Its People* (Norman: University of Oklahoma Press, 1988), 36.

33. Seratt and Ryburn-Lamont, *Historic and Architectural Resources of Route 66*, 17.

34. Bureau of Labor Statistics, "Consumer Price Index CPI Inflation Calculator," http://146.142.4.24/cgi-bin/cpicalc.pl. (accessed June 1, 2006). The exact figure for $25,000 in 1928 dollars was $294,590.60 in 2006 dollars.

35. Tom Teague, Bob Waldmire, and Lon Haldeman, *Searching for 66: The Complete Route 66 Book*, 2nd ed. (Springfield, Illinois: Samizdat House, 1996), 102–7.

36. Kelly and Scott, *Route 66: The Highway and Its People*, 36.

37. Kelly and Scott, *Route 66: The Highway and Its People*, 48.

38. Seratt and Ryburn-Lamont, *Historic and Architectural Resources of Route 66*, 17.

39. U.S. Department of the Interior, National Park Service, *Special Resource Study: Route 66* (Denver: U.S. Department of the Interior, 1995, 8.

40. National Park Service, *Special Resource Study: Route 66*, 11.

41. National Park Service, *Special Resource Study: Route 66*, 15.

42. Michael Karl Witzel, *Route 66 Remembered* (Osceola, WI: Motorbooks International, 1996), 95.

43. Moore and Grauwels, *Route 66: The Illustrated Guidebook to the Mother Road* (Williams, AZ: Roadbook International, 1998), 39.

44. National Park Service, *Special Resource Study: Route 66*, 10.

45. John Steinbeck, *The Grapes of Wrath* (New York: Viking Press, 1939), 128.

46. Michael Azevedo and Patricia Crotty, "Surviving the Dustbowl," The American Experience, http://www.pbs.org/wgbh/amex/dustbowl (accessed May 7, 2006).

47. Thomas Pew Jr., "Route 66, a Ghost Road" *American Heritage*, July 1977, 32.

48. R. Douglas Hurt, *The Dust Bowl: An Agricultural and Social History* (Chicago: Nelson-Hall, 1981), 98.

49. R. Douglas Hurt, "Dust," *American Heritage*, July 1977, 30–31.

50. National Park Service, *Special Resource Study: Route 66*, 15.

51. Interview with Route 66 merchant, September 30, 1998.

52. Helen Hornbeck Tanner, *The Settling of North America: The Atlas of the Great Migrations into North America from the Ice Age to the Present* (New York: Macmillan, 1995), 150.

53. Donald Worster, *Dust Bowl: The Southern Plains in the 1930s* (New York: Oxford University Press, 1979), 58.

54. Steinbeck, *Grapes of Wrath*, 128.

55. Bill Ganzel, *Dust Bowl Descent* (Lincoln: University of Nebraska Press, 1984), 30.

56. Interview with retired Route 66 restaurant owner, September 29, 1998.

57. Tanner, *The Settling of North America*, 150.

58. Kammer, *Historic and Architectural Resources of Route 66*, 60.

59. Kammer, *Historic and Architectural Resources of Route 66*, 54.

60. Kammer, *Historic and Architectural Resources of Route 66*, 53.

61. Seratt and Ryburn-Lamot, *Historic and Architectural Resources of Route 66*, 19.

62. National Park Service, *Special Resource Study: Route 66*, 11.

63. Kammer, *Historic and Architectural Resources of Route 66*, 57.

64. Kammer, *Historic and Architectural Resources of Route 66*, 60.

65. American Automobile Association, "Americans on the Highway," *Tourist Court Journal*, October 1937, 18.

66. Mary Anne Beecher, "The Motel in Builder's Literature and Architectural Publications," in *Roadside America: The Automobile in Design and Culture*, ed. Jan Jennings (Ames: Iowa State University Press, 1990), 116.

67. Paul Lancaster, "The Great American Motel," *American Heritage*, June/July 1982, 116.

68. Liebs, *Main Street to Miracle Mile*, 196.

69. Seratt and Ryburn-Lamot, *Historic and Architectural Resources of Route 66*, 23.

70. Liebs, *Main Street to Miracle Mile*, 27–33.

71. Warren James Belasco, *Americans on the Road: From Autocamp to Motel, 1910–1945* (Cambridge, MA: MIT Press), 169.

72. Lisa Mahar, *American Signs: Form and Meaning on Route 66* (New York: Monacelli Press, 2002), 108.

73. Belasco, "Commercialized Nostalgia," 118.

74. Robert Schweitzer and Michael W. R. Davis, *America's Favorite Homes: Mail-Order Catalogues as a Guide to Popular Early 20th Century Houses* (Detroit MI: Wayne State University Press, 1990), 78.

75. Keith A. Sculle, "Frank Redford's Wigwam Village Chain," in *Roadside America*, 125.

76. Wigwam Motel. "About the Wigwam Village," http://hometown.aol.com/spoolinooo/myhomepage/business.html (accessed May 10, 2006).

77. Kammer, *Historic and Architectural Resources of Route 66*, 18–20.

78. Historic 1930s postcards, author's collection.

79. National Park Service, *Special Resource Study: Route 66*, 16.

80. Seratt and Ryburn-Lamont, *Historic and Architectural Resources of Route 66*, 25.

81. Interview with retired Route 66 restaurant operator, September 29, 1998.

82. Jack Rittenhouse, *A Guide to Highway 66* (Albuquerque: University of New Mexico, 1946), 9.

83. National Park Service, *Special Resource Study: Route 66*, 16.

84. Interview with retired Route 66 gas station operator, September 29, 1998.

85. Interview with retired Route 66 gas station operator, September 29, 1998.

86. Kelly and Scott, *Route 66: The Highway and Its People*, 38.

87. Kammer, *Historic and Architectural Resources of Route 66*, 72.

88. Rittenhouse, *A Guide to Highway 66*, 9.

89. Rittenhouse, *A Guide to Highway 66*, 14, 43, 64, 85, and 103.

90. Seratt and Ryburn-Lamont, *Historic and Architectural Resources of Route 66*, 27.

91. Wallis, *Route 66: The Mother Road*, 23.

92. Kammer, *Historic and Architectural Resources of Route 66*, 74.

93. U.S. Bureau of Census, "Bureau of Census Report on Courts," *Tourist Court Journal*, September 1950, 12.

94. Liebs, *Main Street to Miracle Mile*, 60.

95. This assessment is based on a survey of issues of the *Tourist Court Journal* from the late 1940s and early 1950s.

96. Belasco, "Commercialized Nostalgia," 168.

97. The availability of creature comforts increased after World War II. A sample of statements taken from the backs of historic postcards that advertise their amenities indicate that technological innovations in rooms gained importance in the motel industry on Route 66 and elsewhere.

Amenity	1925–1935	1935–1945	1945–1955	1955–1970
Heat	50%	40%	44%	32%
Pvt. Bath	39%	24%	11%	2.5%
Hot water	11%	16%	7%	1.5%
Cross vent	0%	8%	0%	1.5%
Telephone	0%	8%	18%	27%
Radio	17%	8%	11%	10%
Television	0%	0%	14%	54%
A/C	0%	12%	40%	54%
Carpet	0%	0%	20%	22%
Furnished	6%	8%	0%	0%
Special Furniture	0%	8%	10%	2.5%

The above table shows the percentage of the amenities advertised on motel postcards listed at the top of each column.

98. Historic 1954 postcard, author's collection.

99. Tom Teague, Bob Waldmire, and Lon Haldeman, *Searching for 66* (Springfield, IL: Samizdat House, 1991), 147.

100. Kammer, *Historic and Architectural Resources of Route 66*, 76.

101. Wallis, *Route 66: The Mother Road*, 192.

102. Gladwell Richardson, "Two Guns, Arizona," www.hkhinc.com/arizona/twoguns/tradingpost.htm (accessed October 30, 2006).

103. Witzel, *Route 66 Remembered*, 11–32.

104. Thomas Arthur Repp, *Route 66 : Empires of Amusement* (Lynnwood, Washington: Mock Turtle Press, 1999), 151.

105. Teague, Waldmire, and Haldeman, *Searching for 66*, 113.

106. 1954 Official Map of New Mexico, author's collection.

107. Historic 1953 postcard, author's collection.

108. Historic 1950s postcard, author's collection.

109. Historic postcards, author's collection.

110. Kelly and Scott, *Route 66: The Highway and Its People*, 174.

111. Witzel, *Route 66 Remembered*, 108.

112. The Big Texan Steak Ranch was established in 1959 on Route 66, http://www.bigtexan.com/history.htm (accessed April 12, 2005).

113. Witzel, *Route 66 Remembered*, 42–140.

114. Historic 1950s postcard, author's collection.

115. Repp, *Route 66: Empires of Amusement*, 143.

116. Historic 1950s postcard, author's collection.

117. Barbara Rubin, "Aesthetic Ideology and Urban Design," in *Common Places: Readings in American Vernacular Architecture*, ed. Dell Upton and John Michael Vlach (Athens: University of Georgia Press, 1986), 498.

118. Jim Datsko, "The Spirit of Route 66, the Classic Route 66 TV Series," *Route 66 Magazine*, Winter 1995–96, 40.

119. Witzel, *Route 66 Remembered*, 45.

120. Ca. 1960 canned grape label, Suma Fruit International, Cadiz Valley, California, author's collection.

121. Bill Kinder, in discussion with author, March 18, 2006. Kinder, who bought the Blue Swallow Motel in Tucumcari, New Mexico, in 2005, has an original pack of Route 66 Cigarettes in the vintage cigarette machine that he keeps in the motel's lobby, which he claims dates to the 1960s.

122. eu-cigarettes.net, http://eu-cigarettes.net/index.php?main_page=index&cPath=64_65 (accessed May 15, 2006).

123. Main Street of America Association, *US 66: Main Street of America* (Clinton, OK: Main Street of America Association, 1971), 1–15.

124. Ca. 1965 and ca. 1970 fan postcards (San Francisco, CA: H. S. Cocker Co.), author's collection.

125. *US 66: Main Street of America*, front cover.

126. *US 66: Main Street of America*, back cover.

127. Interview with Route 66 merchant, September 29, 1998.

128. Interview with Route 66 merchant, September 30, 1998.

129. Steinbeck, *The Grapes of Wrath* (1939); Bobby Troup, "Route 66" (1948); the television program, *Route 66* (1960–64); *Route 66 Magazine*; the Route 66 Corridor Study Act of 1990; and the Route 66 Corridor Preservation Act of 1999.

Chapter Three

1. Michael Taylor, director of Route 66 Corridor Preservation Program, in discussion with author, Santa Fe, New Mexico, August 11, 2003. David Kammer, Route 66 historian, in discussion with author, Albuquerque, New Mexico, August 12, 2003.
2. "Bob Dole Could Learn a Thing or Two from Route 66," *The Economist*, July 27,` 1996, 5.
3. Michael Wallis, *Route 66: The Mother Road* (New York: St. Martin's Press, 1990); *Route 66 Magazine, in Memory of Bobby Troup*, collector's edition, summer 1999; Jerry Richard, ed., "Well Known Song Added to Popularity of Route 66," *Route 66 News: Magazine and Newsletter for the Historic Route 66 Association of Arizona*, April 1990, 1; Jerry Richard, ed., "Route 66 in Legend, Song, Film, TV Series, and History," *Route 66 News: Magazine and Newsletter for the Historic Route 66 Association of Arizona*, April 1990, 21.
4. Tom Teague, Bob Waldmire, and Lon Haldeman. *Searching for 66*, 2nd ed. (Springfield, IL: Samizdat House, 1996), 1–2.
5. Constance E. Beaumont, *How Superstore Sprawl Can Harm Communities and What Citizens Can Do About It* (Washington D.C.: National Trust for Historic Preservation, 1994), 3.
6. John Robinson, *Highways and Our Environment* (New York: McGraw Books, 1971), 58.
7. Robinson, *Highways and Our Environment*, 60.
8. Charlton Obburn, "The Motorcar vs. America," *American Heritage*, April 1969, 107.
9. Teri A. Cleeland, "Route 66 Revisited," *Cultural Resource Management* 16.11 (1993): 15.
10. Michael Wallis, "Route 66, the Mother Road" (lecture, Route 66 Expo, Shamrock, TX, October 2, 1998).
11. Betsy Malloy, "California for Visitors: Route 66 in the Southwest," About.com, http://gocalifornia.about.com/cs/route66/a/route66_2.htm (accessed July 12, 2005).
12. Jayne Clark, "A Golden Road's Unlimited Devotion," *USA TODAY*, October 29, 2001, www.usatoday.com/life/travel/leisure/2001/2001–06–29-route66. htm (accessed December 21, 2001; requires subscription).
13. Thomas W. Pew Jr., "Route 66, a Ghost Road," *American Heritage*, July 1977, 26–32.
14. Thomas W. Pew Jr., "Tucumcari Tonight! Requiem for the Last Holdout on Interstate 40," *American West Magazine*, January/February 1980, 35, 62–63.
15. Thomas W. Pew Jr., "Good-bye to Main Street 66, No More Homemade Apple Pie," *American West Magazine*, September/October 1984, 47–51.
16. Teague, Waldmire and Haldeman, *Searching for 66*, 3.
17. As of late 2006, the Arizona group had a membership of nearly 600.
18. Angel and Vilma Delgadillo's Route 66 Gift Shop and Visitor's Center, http://www.route66giftshop.com/main.html (accessed July 11, 2005).
19. Cleeland, "Route 66 Revisited," 16.

20. David Knudson, "Route 66" (lecture, Route 66 Expo, Amarillo, TX, October 3, 1998).
21. Old Town Victorville Property Owners Association, "Presenting Historic and Contemporary Route 66," pamphlet, 1998.
22. U.S. Department of the Interior National Park Service, *Special Resource Study: Route 66* (Washington, D.C., 1995), 12.
23. Route 66 Corridor Preservation Act, Public Law 106-45, 106th Congress, http://www.cr.nps.gov/rt66/PublicLaw106-45.pdf (accessed October 14, 2006).
24. Mohammed Natha, proprietor of the Aztec Motel at 3821 Central Ave., Albuquerque, New Mexico, in discussion with author, August 12, 2003.
25. Route 66 Corridor Preservation Act, Public Law 106-45, Historic Preservation 16 U.S. Code Vol. 461, H.R. 66 1999.
26. National Park Service, "Preserving America's Heritage: History/Significance," http://www.cr.nps.gov/rt66/HistSig/index.htm (accessed October 14, 2006).
27. Greg Smith, "Route 66 Revisited: Preserving the Mother Road," *Society for Commercial Archeology News*, Winter 1999–2000, 3.
28. Greg Smith, "Route 66 Revisited," 4.
29. Greg Smith, "Route 66 Revisited," 5.
30. National Park Service, "Preserving America's Heritage: Program Description," http://www.cr.nps.gov/rt66/prgrm/index.htm (accessed October 14, 2006).
31. Michael Cassity. *Route 66 Corridor National Historic Context Study* (Santa Fe: Route 66 National Corridor Preservation Program, National Trails System Office—Intermountain Region, National Park Service, 2004).
32. *Route 66 News: The Quarterly Newsletter of the Historic Route 66 Association of Arizona*, Winter 1999, 3. Of the 208 foreign visitors reported, 58 came from Germany and 38 from the United Kingdom.
33. Bill Graves, "On Route 66 in Amboy, California," *Trailer Life*, August 1998, 118.
34. Jean Michel, "Welcome French Route 66 Association," *Route 66 News: Magazine and Newsletter for the Historic Route 66 Association of Arizona*, February 1990, 1.
35. Naonori Kohira, "Japan and Interest in Route 66," *Route 66 News: Magazine and Newsletter for the Historic Route 66 Association of Arizona*, March 1990, 22.
36. Estimated membership of a selection of Route 66 associations include the National Historic Route 66 Federation: 1,700 members; the California Historic Route 66 Association: 300 members; Historic Route 66 Association of Arizona: 600 members; Route 66 Association of New Mexico: 320 members; Texas Old Route 66 Association: 320 members; Canadian Route 66 Association: 249 members; Norwegian Route 66 Association: 190 members. These estimates were collected through direct Internet queries to the organizations made by the author, September 5, 2000, and June 1, 2006.
37. National Historic Route 66 Federation Web site, http://www.national66. com (accessed December 28, 2003).

Chapter Four

1. Alana MacDonald, Tom Dean, and Herb Ludwig, "Bye Bye Route 66," http://www.devonsquare.com/discog.htm (accessed February 7, 2006). This was a popular song in 1992.

2. Linda Hutcheon, "Irony, Nostalgia, and the Postmodern," University of Toronto English Library (1998), http://www.library.utoronto.ca/utel/criticism/hutchinp.html (accessed April 6, 2006).

3. Hutcheon, "Irony, Nostalgia, and the Postmodern."

4. Wikipedia, "Nostalgia," *Wikipedia: The Free Encyclopedia*, http://en.wikipedia.org/wiki/Nostalgia (accessed April 6, 2006).

5. Martha Sherrill, "'55 Cadillac on Route 66: Tour Guide to Tad Pierson's American Dream Safari," *Esquire*, August 1995, 36.

6. D. Jeanene Tiner, *Route 66: Mainstreet of America* (Mesa, AZ: Terrell Publishing, 1998), 17.

7. Its official Web site at one point described *Route 66 Magazine* as "the first and only slick, four-color publication written expressly for the Route 66 Roadie. Our stories are a blend of narratives and documentaries that make The Mother Road tick with tales that chronicle the history of an era revolving around a highway which, at one time, was the primary highway from Santa Monica, California to Chicago, Illinois, or vice-versa." This description is no loner available at the magazine's Web site but can be found at http://www.synaptic.bc.ca/CriticalResources/Route-66.htm (accessed October 14, 2006).

8. In 1998, hats and other regalia featuring an "X" that represented the black activist Malcolm X were popular among teenagers.

9. Bob Moore, "Fifties Memories," *Route 66 Magazine*, Fall 1998, 50–51.

10. Jim Cook, "The Summer of '54," *Route 66 Magazine*, Winter 1995–96, 18–19.

11. 11. Jim Datsko, "The Spirit of Route 66, the Classic Route 66 TV Series," *Route 66 Magazine*, Winter 1995–96, 40–42.

12. 12. Jim Datsko, "The Spirit of Route 66," 40–42.

13. Paul Taylor, "How TV Got Its Kicks on Route 66," *Route 66 Magazine*, Summer 2003, 25.

14. 14. Karal Ann Marling, *As Seen on TV: The Visual Culture of Everyday Life in the 1950s* (Cambridge, MA: Harvard University Press, 1997), 5.

15. Marling, *As Seen on TV*, 5.

16. Elaine Tyler May, *Homeward Bound: American Families in the Cold War Era* (New York: Basic Books, 1988), 11.

17. John Greene. "What Was The Kinsey Report? How a Revolutionary 1948 Book Revealed That Most Sex Happens When People Are Alone," http://www.jackinworld.com/library/articles/kinsey.html (accessed March 30, 2006).

18. Tyler May, *Homeward Bound*, 11.

19. University of San Diego Department of History, http://history.sandiego.edu/gen/20th/coldwaro.html (accessed March 30, 2006).

20. University of San Diego Department of History, http://history.sandiego.edu/gen/20th/coldwaro.html (accessed March 30, 2006).

21. U.S. Department of Energy, Department of Environmental Management, http://web.em.doe.gov/timeline/the50s.html (accessed March 30, 2006).
22. u-s-history.com, http://www.u-s-history.com/pages/h3706.html (accessed March 30, 2006).
23. University of San Diego Department of History, http://history.sandiego.edu/gen/20th/coldwaro.html (accessed March 30, 2006).
24. Michael Wallis, lecture, Second Annual International Route 66 Roadie Gathering, Tucumcari, New Mexico, July 10–13, 2003.
25. Michael Wallis, lecture.
26. Michael Wallis, "Route 66: All American Road," *Route 66 New Mexico: A Quarterly Published by the New Mexico Route 66 Association*, Fall 2003, 14–15.
27. Lou Delina, "Kerouac & Cassady: Were These Free Spirits the Original Buz & Tod?" *Route 66 Magazine*, Winter 1995–96, 42–44.
28. Lou Delina, "Kerouac & Cassady," 44.
29. Jack Kerouac, *On the Road* (New York: Viking Press, 1955), 12.
30. Jack Kerouac, *On the Road*, 86.
31. Frank Lloyd Wright, quoted in Bob Lundy, "The Good Life," *Tourism Today: The Quarterly Publication of the San Bernardino County Tourism Development Council*, Spring 1990, 1.
32. John R. Gillis, "Remembering Memory: A Challenge for Public Historians in a Post-National Era," *The Public Historian* 14 (Fall 1992), 91.
33. John R. Gillis, "Remembering Memory," 98.
34. Michael Kammen, *The Mystic Chords of Memory* (New York: Vintage Books, 1993), 535.
35. Bob Garfield, "Air of Authenticity Drives Route 66 Line," *Advertising Age*, August 10, 1998, 29.
36. Bob Garfield, "Air of Authenticity," 29.
37. Kmart Corporation, http://www.kmart.com/catalog/brand.jsp?categoryId=905 (accessed February 7, 2006).
38. John Elmore and Anne E. Smith, "Japanese Use Downtown Kingman for Blue Jean Commercial Filming on Route 66," *Route 66 News: Magazine and Newsletter for the Historic Route 66 Association of Arizona*, November 1990, 16.
39. Kmart designed and copyrighted a red and tan shield as a trademark for Route 66 jeans.
40. Editor of product review, *Cycle*, September 1988, 33–38.
41. Oklahoma Route 66 Association, "Official Oklahoma Route 66 Association Trip Guide," Oklahoma Native Council and the Oklahoma Department of Tourism and Recreation, 1999, 1–98.
42. An Internet search on the Google search engine conducted by the author on December 21, 2001, using the words "Historic Route 66" resulted in 8,620 hits. A search using the same phrase on the same search engine yielded about 24,400 hits on December 28, 2003.
43. Google.com, http://www.google.com (accessed February 7, 2006).
44. Michael Wallis, "Route 66, the Mother Road" (lecture, Route 66 Expo, Shamrock, TX, October 2, 1998). Wallis apparently modified his nostalgic

views of Route 66 as evidenced by his 2003 Tucumcari speech, cited earlier in this chapter.

45. Michael Wallis, *Route 66: The Mother Road* (New York: St. Martin's Press, 1990), 2.

46. Phyllis Evans, in discussion with author, Albuquerque, New Mexico, August 12, 2003.

47. Greg Harrison, "Rediscovering Route 66," *American Motorcyclist: Journal of the American Motorcycle Association*, www.hhjm.com/66/static/highway1. htm (accessed April 27, 2000).

48. Route 66 U.S.A. International Association, www.route66usa.com/info.html (accessed April 27, 2000).

49. Route 66 Association of Illinois, in cooperation with the Illinois Department of Commerce and Community Affairs Bureau of Tourism, *Historic Route 66* (Springfield: Illinois Department of Commerce and Community Affairs Bureau of Tourism, 1998), 2.

50. Holbrook, Arizona, www.arizonaguide.com/cities/holbrook/route66.html (accessed April 27, 2000; site now discontinued but most of the quote appears at http://www.ci.holbrook.az.us/index.asp?Type=B_BASIC&SEC= %7B1B67B8B1-893D-4B51-A2C5-23ACA8794241%7D [accessed October 15, 2006]).

51. Ted Anthony, "History of the Mother Road," *The Spokesman-Review*, Spokane, WA, November 30, 1997, http://www.route66giftshop.com/history .html (accessed October 15, 2006).

52. Tiner, *Route 66: Mainstreet of America*, 1.

53. Steve Wilson, "Two-Lane Vacation: Highway Trip along What Is Left of Route 66 in New Mexico and Arizona Reveals a Bygone Era," *Travel Holiday*, April 1998, 54.

54. Ted Anthony, "History of the Mother Road."

55. Thomas Arthur Repp, *Route 66: The Empires of Amusement* (Lynwood, Washington: Mock Turtle Press, 1999). Repp's book provides an entertaining and informative guide to thirty-three roadside attractions that operated along historic Route 66 when it was in active use as a certified highway.

56. David Kammer, Route 66 historian, in discussion with author, Albuquerque, New Mexico, August 12, 2003.

57. Wallis, *Route 66: The Mother Road*, 1–2.

58. Illinois Route 66 merchant, September 29, 1998.

59. David Kammer, Route 66 historian, in discussion with author, August 12, 2003.

60. Peter Fish, "Canyons, Cozy Dogs, and the Meaning of the West," *Sunset*, December 1998, 18.

61. Tom Snyder, *Route 66: Traveler's Guide and Roadside Companion* (New York: St. Martin's Press, 1990), xvii.

62. David Knudson, "Route 66" (lecture, Route 66 Expo, Amarillo, TX October 3, 1998).

63. Martin Mathis, "Road Trips Revisited—A Route 66 Essay," www.lastbandit. com/rte66pix.html (accessed April 25, 2000).

64. Interview with Route 66 merchants, September 30, 1998.

65. As indicated by author's sample of used historic Route 66 postcards.
66. Historic postcard, author's collection.
67. Historic postcard, author's collection.
68. Historic postcard, author's collection.
69. Historic postcard, author's collection.
70. Jerry McClanahan, "Wish You Were Here," *Route 66 Magazine*, Summer 1999, reproduction of 1957 postcard, 33.
71. McClanahan, "Wish You Were Here," 33.
72. Historic postcard, author's collection.
73. Historic postcard, author's collection.
74. McClanahan, "Wish You Were Here," 34.
75. Of the sixty historic Route 66 postcard card notes sampled, twenty mention the weather, thirteen say they're enjoying their trip (one writer reported not having fun on her trip), twelve commented on the quality of their accommodations, eleven commented on the scenery, seven mentioned natural sites, such as the Petrified Forest, four cited the number of miles they'd gone that day, four mentioned the quality of roads, two reported car repairs, and two mentioned being on Route 66.
76. Work Progress Administration Writer's Program, *Oklahoma: A Guide to the Sooner State* (Washington, D.C.: WPA, 1941).
77. Interview with Route 66 merchant, September 30, 1998.
78. Jerry Richard, "Well Known Song Added to Popularity of Route 66," *Route 66 News: Magazine and Newsletter for the Historic Route 66 Association of Arizona*, March 1990, 21.
79. Interview with Route 66 merchant, September 29, 1998.
80. Chester Henry, quoted in Jon Robinson, *Route 66: Lives on the Road* (Osceola, IL: MBI Publishing Company, 2001), 46.
81. Clyde McCune in Chester Henry in Jon Robinson, *Route 66: Lives on the Road*, 54.
82. "Automobile," *West's Encyclopedia of American Law* (New York: The Gale Group, Inc, 1998), Answers.com http://www.answers.com/topic/automobile (accessed March 28, 2006).
83. U.S. Bureau of Transportation Statistics, http://www.bts.gov/publications/national_transportation_statistics/2005/index.html (accessed March 28, 2006).
84. "Automobile," *West's Encyclopedia of American Law*, http://www.answers.com/topic/automobile (accessed March 28, 2006).
85. Bill Pierce in Jon Robinson, *Route 66 Lives on the Road*, 62–63.
86. Jim Morrison, "An American Prayer: Album Poem Collection," http://www.thedoors.com/band/jim/?fa=poetry1 (accessed March 28, 2006).
87. Michael H. Frisch and Daniel J. Walkowitz, "Introduction," in *Working-Class America: Essays on Labor, Community, and American Society*, ed. Michael H. Frisch and Daniel J. Walkowitz (Urbana: University of Illinois Press, 1996), x.
88. David Lowenthal, *The Past is a Foreign Country* (New York: Cambridge University Press, 1985), 212.
89. Examples of popular books that emphasize personal accounts and

individual sites include *Route 66 Remembered* by Michael Karl Witzel, *Searching for 66* by Tom Teague, Bob Waldmire, and Lon Haldeman, and *Route 66: The Mother Road* by Michael Wallis.

90. Norman F. Cantor, *Inventing the Middle Ages: The Lives, Works, and Ideas of the Great Medievalists of the Twentieth Century* (New York: William Morrow, 1991).

91. Guy Randall, "Shadows of Old Route 66: The Route 66 Primer, a Brief History." http://www.theroadwanderer.net/route66.htm (accessed July 12, 2005).

92. Several Route 66 businesspeople described Route 66 as being crowded in the 1950s. Traffic counts cited in chapter 3 also support this assertion.

93. David Macaulay, *Motel of the Mysteries* (New York: Houghton Mifflin Company, 1979), 1–140.

94. Chip Lord, "Ant Farm's Cadillac Ranch: About the Ranch." http://www.libertysoftware.be/cml/cadillacranch/ranch/crabtr.htm (accessed July 12, 2005).

95. "Built along the tattered remains of historic Route 66, the cars were meant to represent the 'Golden Age' of American automobiles," Kathy Weisner writes in "Lone Star Legends: The Cadillac Ranch in Amarillo, Texas," http://www.legendsofamerica.com/TX-CadillacRanch.html (accessed July 12, 2005).

96. Suzanne Gamboa, "Cadillac Ranch, Only Buried Halfway, Cars' Meaning Goes Much Deeper," *The Austin American Statesmen*, 16 May 1994, sec. 1A, 2.

97. Wallis, *Route 66: The Mother Road*, 2.

98. CitiVU, Route 66 Museum and Rancho Cucamonga Visitor's Center, www.citivu.com/rc/rte66 (accessed September 25, 1997; site now discontinued).

99. Martin Mathis, "Route 66 Road Trip," www.lastbandit.com/rte66pix.html (accessed April 27, 2000).

100. Wallis, *Route 66: The Mother Road*, 26.

101. Joyce Appleby, *Telling the Truth About History* (New York: W. W. Norton, 1994), 201.

102. Todd Gitlin, "Postmodernism: Roots and Politics, What Are They Talking About?" *Dissent* (Winter 1989), 100.

103. Steven Best and Douglas Kellner, *Postmodern Theory: Critical Interrogations* (New York: Guilford Press, 1991), 4–5.

104. Examples of "glass boxes" include the Seagram Building by Mies van der Rohe and Phillip Johnson, 1954–58, in New York City and the Lever House by Skidmore Owings and Merrill, 1952, also in New York.

105. Charles A. Jencks, *The Language of Post-Modern Architecture* (New York: Rizzoli Publishers, 1977), 8.

106. Robert Venturi, Denise Scott Brown, and Steven Izenour, *Learning from Las Vegas* (Cambridge, MA: MIT Press, 1977).

107. Tom Wolfe, *From Bauhaus to Our House* (Toronto: McGraw Hill, 1981), 104.

108. Robert Venturi (lecture, Association for Preservation Technology annual conference, Philadelphia, PA, October 2000).

109. John Storey, *An Introduction to Cultural Theory and Popular Culture* (Athens:

University of Georgia Press, 1998), 169–88. This source provides a general discussion of the wide impact of postmodernism on Western culture.

110. Examples taken from recent television commercials played during the Super Bowl. These can be found at "Oldest and largest TV Commercial Library since 1975," http://www.usatvads.com (accessed February 14, 2006).

111. Robert Venturi, lecture.

Chapter Five

1. On the regulations involving underground fuel storage tanks, see Charles Bartsch, Elizabeth Collaton, and Edith Pepper, *Development: A Resource Book on Environmental Cleanup and Economic Development Opportunities* (Washington, D.C.: Northeast-Midwest Institute, 1996), http://www.nemw.org/cmclean1.htm (accessed December 30, 2003).

2. Ron Jackson, "Route 66 Lovers Fear Replacement of Original Road," *The Daily Oklahoman* (Oklahoma City), September 8, 1999, sec. A, 6.

3. Michael Taylor, director of Route 66 Corridor Preservation Program, in discussion with author, Santa Fe, New Mexico, August 11, 2003.

4. Michael Taylor, in discussion with author, August 11, 2003.

5. A "building" shelters human activity on a regular basis, whereas a "structure" is any man-made constructed artifact that can be found in the landscape. An example of a building is a warehouse where at least a few people work and examples of structures include cell towers and bridges.

6. Gary L. Hume and W. Brown Morton III, *Secretary of the Interior's Standards for Rehabilitation and Guidelines for Rehabilitating Historic Buildings*, U.S Department of the Interior, National Park Service (Washington, D.C.: U.S. Department of the Interior, 1992).

7. Historic postcard, author's collection.

8. Charles A. Birnbaum and Christine Capella Peters, *The Secretary of the Interior's Standards for the Treatment of Historic Properties with Guidelines for the Treatments of Cultural Landscapes*, National Park Service, Cultural Resource Stewardship and Partnerships, Heritage Preservation Services Historic Landscape Initiative (Washington, D.C.: U.S. Department of the Interior 1995), 4.

9. David Knudson, "Director's Notes," *Route 66 Federation News*, Summer 1998, 2.

10. Alfred Runte, quoted in Peter Fish, "Canyons, Cozy Dogs, and the Meaning of the West," *Sunset*, December 1998, 19.

11. Waldmire's visitor's center was purchased by another Route 66 enthusiast and continues to operate for Route 66 tourists as of this writing.

12. Bob Waldmire, quoted in Peter Fish, "Canyons, Cozy Dogs, and the Meaning of the West," by Peter Fish, *Sunset*, December 1998, 19.

13. David Kammer, Route 66 historian, in discussion with author, Albuquerque, New Mexico, August 12, 2003.

14. Greg Smith, the National Register coordinator at the Texas Historical Commission, and the author developed this plan in July 2001. The Texas Historical Commission is the state historic preservation office of Texas.

15. The entire National Register of Historic Places can be found on a searchable database at www.nps.gov.
16. In order for a property or a district (a distinct geographical area, which contains multiple buildings and/or structures) to be eligible for listing on the National Register, it usually has to be at least fifty years old and have historic value because it directly meets one or more of the following criteria: A) historic events occurred there, B) famous or historically-significant people lived or visited there, C) it possesses significant or distinctive architecture, D) it potentially could yield significant archeological information.
17. Michael Cassity, *Corridor National Historic Context Study* (Santa Fe: Route 66 National Corridor Preservation Program, National Trails System Office—Intermountain Region, National Park Service, 2004).
18. Although properties deemed eligible for listing in the National Register by a state historic preservation office receive the same protection as listed properties, listing removes any doubt that the property will be considered historic if it becomes endangered by a federal undertaking.
19. Advisory Council for Historic Preservation, "Section 106 Regulations Users Guide," http://www.achp.gov/usersguide.html (accessed October 17, 2006).
20. This statement is based on the author's experience of working closely with Section 106 in Texas as an employee of the Texas Department of Transportation and at the Texas Historical Commission.
21. Section 4(f) also applies to parks and wildlife sanctuaries.
22. A detailed section 4(f) policy paper provided by the Federal Highway Administration can be found at http://environment.fhwa.dot.gov/projdev/4fpolicy.htm#3.
23. "The Bush Administration's transportation reauthorization bill, known as SAFETEA, would eviscerate the protections provided by Section 4(f). While SAFETEA would retain the existing 'no feasible and prudent alternative'" language, it also contains so many exemptions and redefinitions that road-builders could easily plow straight through 4(f)." National Trust for Historic Preservation, "Issues and Initiatives: Transportation," http://www.nationaltrust.org/issues/transportation/index.html (accessed December 30, 2003; document no longer available). "The United States Senate adopted . . . its version of the transportation reauthorization bill, which was passed on February 12, 2004. The House of Representatives also passed its version of the transportation reauthorization bill on April 2, which includes language on Section 4(f). While it is not as complete in its protections for Section 4(f) as the Voinovich amendment in the Senate version, it is an improvement over the Administration's proposal for Section 4(f)," http://www.nationaltrust.org/issues/transportation/index.html (accessed July 14, 2005; document no longer available).
24. Olivia Fagerberg, tax credit coordinator, Texas Historical Commission, in discussion with author, May 2000.
25. Mary Alice Robbins, "Area Towns Get in Proposal for Improvements," *Amarillo Globe-News*, January 26, 2000, http://amarillo.com/stories/012600/tex_area.shtml (accessed October 17, 2000; registration required). Shamrock received $1,746,864 in federal funds to rehabilitate the tower station.

26. The city of San Antonio, Texas, has such an ordinance. The only short-coming is that there has been opposition to the creation of new National Register districts by property owners, resulting in fewer districts than there might have been in that city.

27. ARCHITEXAS, Architecture, Planning, and Historic Preservation, Inc., *Tower Station and U-Drop Inn, Shamrock, Texas: Historic Structure Report & Restoration Master Plan* (Dallas: ARCHITEXAS, 2000), 2.

28. Teri A. Cleeland, "Route 66 Revisited," *Cultural Resource Management* 16.11 (1993): 15–18.

29. An Internet search revealed that sixty-seven sites associated with Route 66 have been individually listed in the National Register. Of these eight were in Arizona, one was in Illinois, thirty-four were in New Mexico, twenty-three were in Oklahoma, and one was in Texas. Property types listed included motels, gas stations, cafés, trading posts, auto dealerships, highway segments, bridges, a tire store, and bakery, www.nps.gov (accessed January 10, 2001).

30. National Register data, www.nps.gov (accessed July 14, 2005); http://www.cr.nps.gov/rt66/ (accessed July 14, 2005).

31. U.S. Congress. Route 66 Corridor Preservation Act, Public Law 106-45, Historic Preservation 16 USC 461, H.R. 66 1999.

32. Route 66 Corridor Preservation Act.

33. National Park Service, Route 66 Corridor Preservation Program home page, www.cr.nps.gov/rt66/index.htm (accessed June 13, 2005).

34. Route 66 Corridor Preservation Program home page.

35. Bill Kinder, in discussion with author, Tucumcari, New Mexico, March 19, 2006.

36. Michael Taylor, director of Route 66 Corridor Preservation Program, in discussion with author, Santa Fe, New Mexico, August 11, 2003.

37. David Gaines and Art Gomez, "Perspectives on Route 66," *Cultural Resource Management* 16.11 (1993): 23.

38. ARCHITEXAS, *Tower Station and U-Drop Inn, Shamrock, Texas*, 3.

39. Trailnet, http://www.trailnet.org (accessed October 17, 2006). This is a non-profit organization that was founded in 1988 to promote and develop the St. Louis Riverfront Trail. It led the renovation of the historic bridge as a pedestrian and bicycle path; the project was begun in 1997 and completed in 1999.

40. HGTV, RestoreAmerica, http://www.hgtv.com/hgtv/rm_restoration_homes _areas/article/0,1797,HGTV_3787_1381983,00.html (accessed May 17, 2006).

41. Site visit by author, 1998.

42. Brenda Colladay, museum and photograph curator at the Grand Ole Opry, in discussion with author, 1998. Colladay reported seeing a large historic motel in Lawrence, Kansas, that was being used as a year-round flea market, with each vendor occupying a room.

43. Janet Goukas, "How the Aztec Motel Cleaned up It's [*sic*] Act," *Crosswinds*, August 1998, 8. "Aztec Motel Fact Sheet," distributed by Mohammed Natha.

44. Michael Taylor, director of Route 66 Corridor Preservation Program, in discussion with author, Santa Fe, New Mexico, August 11, 2003.

45. Scenic America, *Scenic Byways: Preserving a Part of America's Heritage*, pamphlet, 1–2.

46. Rand McNally and Company, *State Farm Road Atlas, United States, Canada, Mexico* (Skokie, IL: Rand McNally and Company, 2001), 8.

47. Municipalities and state legislators have the power to limit or prohibit billboards. Such laws should be encouraged on Route 66, not for vernacular billboards directing motorists to Route 66 attractions but for the large, generic billboards that corporate advertisers place along highways to promote such products as new cars.

48. Scenic America, *Scenic Byways: Preserving a Part of America's Heritage*, 2.

49. Peter H. Brink, "Livable Communities and Historic Transportation Corridors," *Cultural Resource Management* 16.11 (1993): 52–53.

50. Scenic America, *Scenic Byways: Preserving a Part of America's Heritage*, 2.

Summary and Conclusion

1. El Rancho Hotel and Motel, http://www.elranchohotel.com (accessed May 15, 2006). The list of movies filmed near Gallup and Route 66 includes: *The Bad Man*, an MGM film starring Wallace Berry and Ronald Reagan in 1940; *Sundown*, a Wanger film starring Gene Tierney in 1941; *Desert Song*, starring Dennis Morgan in 1942; *Song Of The Nile*, starring Maria Montez and Jon Hall in 1944; *Four Faces West* and *Colorado Territory*, both starring Joel McCrea in 1947–48; *Streets of Laredo*, starring William Holden and William Bendix in 1948; *Rocky Mountain*, starring Errol Flynn in 1950; *Big Carnival*, starring Kirk Douglas in 1950; *Raton Pass*, starring Dennis Morgan in 1951; *New Mexico*, starring Lew Ayres in 1950; *Fort Defiance*, starring Dane Clark in 1950; *Fort Massacre*, starring Joel McCrea in 1957; *A Distant Trumpet*, starring Troy Donahue and Suzanne Pleshette in 1963; *The Hallelujah Trail*, starring Burt Lancaster and Lee Remick in 1964.

2. Texas Route 66, "Legends of America," Texas Route 66 Association, http://www.theroadwanderer.net/66Texas/route66TX.htm (accessed July 15, 2005).

Bibliography

Advisory Council for Historic Preservation. "Section 106 Regulations Users Guide." http://www.achp.gov/usersguide.html.

Ahlgren, Carol. "The Lincoln Highway." *Cultural Resource Management* 19.9 (1996): 16–17.

American Automobile Association. "Americans on the Highway." *Tourist Court Journal,* October 1937, 18.

Anderson, William T. "Wall Drug-South Dakota's Tourist Emporium." *American West,* August/September 1985, 72–76.

Andrews, J. J. C. *The Well-Built Elephant and Other Road Attractions: A Tribute to American Eccentricity.* New York: Congdon and Weed Inc., 1984.

Anthony, Ted. "History of the Mother Road." *The Spokesman-Review* (Spokane, WA), November 30, 1997. http://route66giftshop.com/history.html.

Appleby, Joyce. *Telling the Truth about History.* New York: W. W. Norton, 1994.

ARCHITEXAS, Architecture, Planning, and Historic Preservation, Inc. *Tower Station and U-Drop Inn, Shamrock, Texas: Historic Structure Report & Restoration Master Plan.* Dallas: ARCHITEXAS, 2000.

Azevedo, Michael, and Patricia Crotty. "Surviving the Dustbowl." The American Experience, http://www.pbs.org/wgbh/amex/dustbowl.

Bartsch, Charles, Elizabeth Collaton, and Edith Pepper. *Development: A Resource Book on Environmental Cleanup and Economic Development Opportunities.* Washington, D.C.: Northeast-Midwest Institute, 1996. http://www.nemw.org/cmclean1.htm.

Beaumont, Constance E. *How Superstore Sprawl Can Harm Communities and*

What Citizens Can Do about It. Washington, D.C.: National Trust for Historic Preservation, 1994.

Beecher, Mary Anne. "The Motel in Builder's Literature and Architectural Publications." In *Roadside America: The Automobile in Design and Culture*, edited by Jan Jennings, 115–24. Ames: Iowa State University Press, 1990.

Belasco, Warren James. *Americans on the Road: From Autocamp to Motel, 1910– 1945*. Cambridge, MA: MIT Press, 1979.

———. "Commercialized Nostalgia, the Origins of the Roadside Strip." In *The Automobile and American Culture*, edited by David L. Lewis and Laurence Goldstein, 105–22. Ann Arbor: University of Michigan Press, 1983.

Berke, Arnold. "Drawing from the Desert, Architect Mary Colter Told Stories in Stone." *Preservation*, Summer 1997, 39–42.

Best, Steven, and Douglas Kellner. *Postmodern Theory: Critical Interrogations*. New York: Guilford Press, 1991.

Birnbaum, Charles A., and Christine Capella Peters. *The Secretary of the Interior's Standards for the Treatment of Historic Properties with Guidelines for the Treatments of Cultural Landscapes*. National Park Service, Cultural Resource Stewardship and Partnerships, Heritage Preservation Services Historic Landscape Initiative. Washington, D.C.: U.S. Department of the Interior, 1995.

Blake, Kevin S. "Zane Grey and Images of the American West." *The Geographic Review*, April 1995, 202–13.

Brink, Peter H. "Livable Communities and Historic Transportation Corridors." *Cultural Resource Management* 16.11 (1993): 52–53.

Bureau of Labor Statistics. "Consumer Price Index CPI Inflation Calculator." http://146.142.4.24/cgi-bin/cpicalc.pl.

Cantor, Norman F. *Inventing the Middle Ages: The Lives, Works, and Ideas of the Great Medievalists of the Twentieth Century*. New York: William Morrow, 1991.

Cassity, Michael. *Route 66 Corridor National Historic Context Study*. Santa Fe: Route 66 National Corridor Preservation Program, National Trails System Office—Intermountain Region, National Park Service, 2004.

Catlin, George. *North American Indians: Being Letters and Notes on Their Manners, Customs, and Conditions, Written During Eight Years' Travel Amongst the Wildest Tribes of North America, 1832–1839*. London: George Catlin, 1880.

CitiVU. "Route 66 Museum and Rancho Cucamonga Visitor's Center," www.citivu.com/rc/rte66; site now discontinued.

Clark, Jayne. "A Golden Road's Unlimited Devotion" *USA TODAY* (Washington D.C.), October 29, 2001. www.usatoday.com/life/travel/leisure/2001/2001– 06–29-route66.htm (subscription required).

Cleeland, Teri A. "Route 66 Revisited." *Cultural Resource Management* 16.11 (1993): 15–18.

Collins, Reba Neighbors. "Just Plain Will." *The Quill*, May 1990, 44–47.

Cook, Richard. "The Summer of '54." *Route 66 Magazine*, Winter 1995–96, 18–19.

Darton, N. H. "The Southwest, Its Splendid Natural Resources, Agricultural

Wealth, and Scenic Beauty." *National Geographic Magazine*, August 21, 1910, 643–44.

Datsko, Jim. "The Spirit of Route 66, the Classic Route 66 TV Series." *Route 66 Magazine*, Winter 1995–96, 40–42.

Delina, Lou. "Kerouac & Cassady: Were These Free Spirits the Original Buz & Tod?" *Route 66 Magazine*, Winter 1995–96, 42–44.

Derry, Anne, Ward H. Jandi, Carol D. Shull, and Jan Thorman. Revised by Patricia L. Parker, 1985. "Guidelines for Local Surveys: A Basis for Preservation Planning: National Register Bulletin 24." Washington D.C.: U.S. Department of the Interior, National Park Service, 1977.

Dilworth, Leah. *Imagining Indians in the Southwest: Persistent Visions of a Primitive Past*. Washington, D.C.: Smithsonian Press, 1996.

Dilworth, Leah. "Tourists and Indians in Fred Harvey's Southwest." In *Seeing and Being Seen: Tourism in the American West*, edited by David M. Wrobel and Patrick T. Long, 142–64. Lawrence: University Press of Kansas, 2001.

Durham, Michael S. "Landmarks on the Rim." *American Heritage*, April 1996, 137–44.

Economist, The. "Bob Dole Could Learn a Thing or Two from Route 66." July 27, 1996.

Elkinton, Steve. "CRM and the National Trails System." *Cultural Resource Management* 20.11 (1997): 3–5.

Elmore, John and Anne E Smith. "Japanese Use Downtown Kingman for Blue Jean Commercial Filming on Route 66." *Route 66 News: Magazine and Newsletter for the Historic Route 66 Association of Arizona*, November 1990, 16.

eu-cigarettes.net. http://eu-cigarettes.net/index.php?main_page=index&cPath =64_65.

Fairchild, Hoxie Neale. *The Noble Savage: A Study in Romantic Naturalism*. New York: Russell and Russell, 1961.

Fish, Peter. "Canyons, Cozy Dogs, and the Meaning of the West." *Sunset*, December 1998, 18–20.

Frisch, Michael H., and Daniel J. Walkowitz, eds. *Working-Class America: Essays on Labor, Community, and American Society*. Urbana: University of Illinois Press, 1996.

Gaines, David, and Art Gomez. "Perspectives on Route 66." *Cultural Resource Management* 16.11 (1993): 21–23.

Gamboa, Suzanne. "Cadillac Ranch: Only Buried Halfway, Cars' Meaning Goes Much Deeper." *The Austin American Statesmen*, May 16, 1994.

Ganzel, Bill. *Dust Bowl Descent*. Lincoln: University of Nebraska Press, 1984.

Garfield, Bob. "Air of Authenticity Drives Route 66 Line." *Advertising Age*, August 10, 1998, 29.

Gillis, John R. "Remembering Memory: A Challenge for Public Historians in a Post-National Era." *The Public Historian* 14 (Fall 1992): 91.

Gitlin, Todd. "Postmodernism: Roots and Politics, What Are They Talking About?" *Dissent*, Winter 1989, 100–105.

Glassberg, David. "Monuments and Memories." *American Quarterly* 43 (March 1991): 149.

Goodman, David. "Postmodernism and History." *American Studies International* 45 (February 1993): 21–29.

Goukas, Janet. "How the Aztec Motel Cleaned up It's [sic] Act." *Crosswinds*, August 1998, 8.

Gowans, Alan. *Styles and Types of North American Architecture: Social Function and Cultural Expression*. New York: Harper Collins, 1992.

Graves, Bill. "On Route 66 in Amboy, California." *Trailer Life*, August 1998, 118–19.

Greene, John. "What Was The Kinsey Report? How a Revolutionary 1948 Book Revealed That Most Sex Happens When People Are Alone." http://www.jackinworld.com/library/articles/kinsey.html.

Grosvenor, Gilbert H. "The Land of the Best." *National Geographic Magazine*, April 24, 1916, 328–35.

Harrison, Greg. "Rediscovering Route 66." *American Motorcyclist: Journal of the American Motorcycle Association*. www.hhjm.com/66/static/highway1.html.

Heath, Duncan, and Judy Boreham. *Introducing Romanticism*. Cambridge: Icon Books, 2000.

Historic Postcards depicting sites on Route 66 and other historic highways, 1910–1970, author's collection.

Historic Route 66 Association. "Visitors." *Route 66 News: The Quarterly Newsletter of the Arizona Route 66 Association*, Winter 1999, 3.

Hokanson, Drake. *The Lincoln Highway: Main Street across America*. Iowa City: University of Iowa Press, 1988.

Holland, Harry. *Traveler's Architecture*. London: George G. Harrap and Co., 1971.

Holbrook, Arizona. http://www.ci.holbrook.az.us/index.asp?Type=B_BASIC&SEC=%7B1B67B8B1-893D-4B51-A2C5-23ACA8794241%7D.

Hudman, Lloyd E. "Tourism and the West." *Journal of the West*, July 1994, 67–76.

Hurt, R. Douglas. "Dust." *American Heritage*, July, 1977, 30–31.

———. *The Dust Bowl: An Agricultural and Social History*. Chicago: Nelson-Hall, 1981.

Interrrante, Joseph. "The Road to Autopia." In *The Automobile and American Culture*, edited by David L. Lewis and Lawrence Goldstein, 94–105. Ann Arbor: University of Michigan Press, 1983.

Jackson, Ron. "Route 66 Lovers Fear Replacement of Original Road." *The Daily Oklahoman* (Oklahoma City), September 8, 1999.

Jakle, John A. *The Tourist: Travel in Twentieth-Century North America*. Lincoln: University of Nebraska Press, 1985.

———, and Keith Sculle. *The Gas Station in America*. Baltimore: Johns Hopkins University Press, 1994.

Jencks, Charles A. *The Language of Post-Modern Architecture*. New York: Rizzoli Publishers, 1977.

Jones, Billy M. *Health Seekers in the Southwest, 1817–1900*. Norman: University of Oklahoma Press, 1967.

Jones, Dwayne. "What's New with the Pig Stands—Not the Pig Sandwich!" *Cultural Resource Management* 19.9 (1996): 18–20.

Kammen, Michael. *The Mystic Chords of Memory*. New York: Vintage Books, 1993.

Kammer, David J. *Historic and Architectural Resources of Route 66 across New Mexico 1926–1956*. National Register of Historic Places Multiple Property Documentation Form. Washington, D.C.: National Park Service, 1993.

Kelly, Susan Croce, and Quinta Scott. *Route 66: The Highway and its People*. Norman: University of Oklahoma Press, 1988.

Kerouac, Jack. *On the Road*. New York: Viking Press, 1955.

Kinder, Bill. Interview with author, March 18, 2006.

Klein, Kerwin L. "Frontier Products: Tourism, Consumerism, and the Southwestern Public Lands, 1890–1990." *Pacific Historical Review* 62 (February 1993): 45–48.

Knudson, David. "Director's Notes." *Route 66 Federation News*, Summer 1998, 2.

———. "Route 66." Lecture, Route 66 Exposition, Amarillo, Texas, October 3, 1998.

Kohira, Naonori. "Japan and Interest in Route 66." *Route 66 News: Magazine and Newsletter for the Historic Route 66 Association of Arizona*, March 1990, 22.

Lamar, Howard Roberts. *The Far Southwest, 1846–1912: A Territorial History*. London: Yale University Press, 1966.

Lancaster, Paul. "The Great American Motel." *American Heritage*, June/July 1982, 101–8.

Liebs, Chester H. *Main Street to Miracle Mile: American Roadside Architecture*. Baltimore: Johns Hopkins University Press, 1995.

Lieder, Michael, and Jake Page. *Wild Justice: The People of Geronimo vs. the United States*. New York: Random House, 1997.

Limerick, Patricia Nelson. *The Legacy of Conquest: The Unbroken Past of the American West*. New York: W. W. Norton, 1987.

Lincoln Highway Association. *The Complete Official Road Guide to the Lincoln Highway*. Sacramento: Pleiades Press, 1984.

Lincoln Highway Association. *The Lincoln Highway: The Story of a Crusade that Made Transportation History*. New York: Dodd, Mead and Company, 1935.

Lowenthal, David. *The Past is a Foreign Country*. New York: Cambridge University Press, 1985.

Lukacs, John. "From Camelot to Abilene." *American Heritage*, February 1981, 55–57.

Lummis, Charles F. *The Land of Poco Tiempo*. New York: Charles Scribner's Sons, 1893. Reprint, New York: Charles Scribner's Sons, 1913.

Lundy, Bob. "The Good Life." *Tourism Today: The Quarterly Publication of the San Bernardino County Tourism Development Council*, Spring 1990, 1.

Lynd, Robert, and Helen Lynd. *Middletown: A Study in Modern American Culture*. New York: Harcourt, Brace and World, 1929.

Macaulay, David. *Motel of the Mysteries*. New York: Houghton Mifflin Company, 1979.

MacDonald, Alana, Tom Dean, and Herb Ludwig. "Bye Bye Route 66." http://www.devonsquare.com/discog.htm.

Mahar, Lisa. *American Signs: Form and Meaning on Route 66*. New York: Monacelli Press, 2002.

Main Street of America Association. *US 66: Main Street of America.* Clinton, OK: Main Street of America Association, 1971.

Malcolm, Andrew S., and Mark McGarrity. *U.S. 1, America's Original Main Street.* New York: St. Martin's Press, 1991.

Malloy, Betsy. "California for Visitors: Route 66 in the Southwest," About.com, http://gocalifornia.about.com/cs/route66/a/route66_2.htm.

Margolies, John. *The End of the Road.* New York: Viking Press, 1981.

Marling, Karal Ann. *As Seen on TV: The Visual Culture of Everyday Life in the 1950s.* Cambridge, MA: Harvard University Press, 1997.

———. *The Colossus of Roads, Myth and Symbol along the American Highway.* Minneapolis: University of Minnesota Press, 1984.

Marsden, M. T. "The Popular Western Novel as a Cultural Artifact." *Arizona and the West,* Spring 1978, 205–10.

Mathis, Martin. "Road Trips Revisited—A Route 66 Essay." www.lastbandit.com/rte66pix.html.

May, Elaine Tyler. *Homeward Bound: American Families in the Cold War Era.* New York: Basic Books, 1988.

McCarthy, Joe. "The Lincoln Highway." *American Heritage,* June 1974, 32–38.

McClanahan, Jerry. "Wish You Were Here." *Route 66 Magazine,* Summer 1999, 32–38.

McCloskey, Robert. *Homer Price.* New York: Scholastic Book Services, 1973.

Metz, Leon C. *Roadside History of Texas.* Missoula, MT: Mountain Press Publishing, 1994.

Michel, Jean. "Welcome French Route 66 Association." *Route 66 News: The Quarterly Newsletter of the Historic Route 66 Association of Arizona,* February 1990, 1–3.

Mitchell, Guy Eliot. "A New National Park." *National Geographic Magazine,* March 21, 1910, 215–24.

Moore, Bob. "Fifties Memories." *Route 66 Magazine,* Fall1998, 50–51.

———, and Patrick Grauwels. *Route 66: The Illustrated Guidebook to the Mother Road.* Williams, AZ: Roadbook International, 1998.

Morgan, Howard E. *The Motel Industry in the United States: Small Business in Transition.* Tucson: The Bureau of Business and Public Research, University of Arizona, 1964.

Murkowski, Frank H. "The Rte. 66 of American Recreation." *Christian Science Monitor,* December 9, 1997, 18.

Nabokov, Vladimir. *Lolita.* New York: Putnam, 1955.

Natha, Mohammed. Interview with author, August 12, 2003.

National Park Service, Denver Service Center. *American Discovery Trail, National Trail Feasibility Study.* Denver, CO: National Park Service, 1995.

National Register of Historic Places, United States Department of the Interior. http://www.cr.nps.gov/nr.

New Mexico State Highway Department. *New Mexico Official Road Map.* Santa Fe: New Mexico State Highway Department, 1954.

Obburn, Charlton. "The Motorcar vs. America." *American Heritage,* April 1969, 104–10.

Oklahoma Route 66 Association. *Official Oklahoma Route 66 Association Trip*

Guide. Oklahoma City: Oklahoma Native Council and the Oklahoma Department of Tourism and Recreation, 1999.

Old Town Victorville Property Owners Association. *Presenting Historic and Contemporary Route 66.* Pamphlet, 1998.

Padget, Martin. "Travel, Exoticism, and the Writing of Region: Charles Fletcher Lummis and the Creation of the Southwest." *Journal of the Southwest,* Autumn 1995, 422–33.

Patton, Phil. "America's Home Away from Home is Still a Good Motel." *Smithsonian,* March 1986, 126–37.

Pew, Thomas W., Jr. "Good-bye to Main Street 66, No More Homemade Apple Pie." *American West Magazine,* September/October 1984, 47–51.

———. "Route 66, a Ghost Road." *American Heritage,* July 1977, 26–32.

———. "Tucumcari Tonight: Requiem for the Last Holdout on Interstate 40." *American West Magazine,* January/February 1980, 62–63.

Porter, Kenneth W. "African Americans in the Cattle Industry, 1860s-1880s." In *Peoples of Color in the American West,* edited By Sucheng Chan, Douglas Daniels, Mario T. Garcia, and Terry P. Wilson. Toronto: Heath and Company, 1994.

Preston, Howard Lawrence. *Dirt Roads to Dixie: Accessibility and Modernization in the South, 1885–1935.* Knoxville: University of Tennessee Press, 1991.

Puzo, Rita A. "Route 66: A Ghost Road Geography." MA thesis, California State University, 1988.

Randall, Guy. "Shadows of Old Route 66: The Route 66 Primer, a Brief History." http://www.theroadwanderer.net/route66.htm.

Rand McNally and Company. *State Farm Road Atlas, United States, Canada, Mexico.* Skokie, IL: Rand McNally and Company, 2001.

Repp, Thomas Arthur. *Route 66: The Empires of Amusement.* Lynwood, WA: Mock Turtle Press, 1999.

Richard, Jerry. "Route 66 in Legend, Song, Film, TV Series, and History." *Route 66 News: Magazine and Newsletter for the Historic Route 66 Association of Arizona,* April 1990, 21.

———. "Well Known Song Added to Popularity of Route 66." *Route 66 News: Magazine and Newsletter for the Historic Route 66 Association of Arizona,* April 1990, 21.

Rittenhouse, Jack. *A Guide to Highway 66.* Los Angeles: J. D. Rittenhouse, 1946. Facsimile edition, Albuquerque: University of New Mexico Press, 1989.

Roach, Steven. "Classicizing America's Indian in the Mid-Nineteenth Century: James Longacre's Indian Cent." History of art honors thesis, University of Michigan, May 2002. http://www.michigancoinclub.org/classicizing.htm.

Robbins, Mary Alice. "Area Towns Get in Proposal for Improvements." *Amarillo Globe-News,* January 26, 2000. http://amarillo.com/stories/012600/tex_area.shtml (registration required).

Robbins, Peggy. "Will Rogers: The Immortal Cherokee Kid." *American History Illustrated,* July 1974, 6.

Robinson, Jon. *Route 66: Lives on the Road.* Osceola, IL: MBI Publishing Company, 2001.

Robinson, John. *Highways and Our Environment*. New York: McGraw Books, 1971.

Rosaldo, Renato. *Culture and Truth: The Remaking of Social Analysis*. Boston: Beacon Press, 1993.

Rose, Mark H. *Interstate: Express Highway Politics, 1941–1956*. Lawrence: The Regents Press of Kansas, 1979.

Rothman, Hal. *Preserving Different Pasts: The American National Monuments*. Urbana: University of Illinois Press, 1989.

Rousseau, Jean Jacques. *Discourse on Inequality*. In *The Noble Savage: A Study in Romantic Naturalism*. London: Hoxie Neale Fairchild, 1794. Reprint, New York: Russell and Russell, 1961.

Route 66 Association of Arizona. *Route 66 News: The Quarterly Newsletter of the Historic Route 66 Association of Arizona*, Winter 1999, 3.

Route 66 Association of Illinois, in cooperation with the Illinois Department of Commerce and Community Affairs Bureau of Tourism. *Historic Route 66*. Springfield: Route 66 Association of Illinois, 1998.

Route 66 U.S.A. International Association. www.route66usa.com.

Rubin, Barbara. "Aesthetic Ideology and Urban Design." In *Common Places: Readings in American Vernacular Architecture*, edited by Dell Upton and John Michael Vlach, 482–507. Athens: University of Georgia Press, 1986.

Runte, Alfred. "Promoting the Golden West: Advertising and the Railroad." *California History*, Spring 1991, 63–75.

Savage, Beth L. "Road-related Resources Listed in the National Register." *Cultural Resource Management* 19.9 (1996): 13.

Savage, William W., Jr. *Cowboy Life: Reconstructing an American Myth*. Norman: University of Oklahoma Press, 1975.

Scenic America. *Corridor Management Plans: Developing Plans for Scenic Byways*. Pamphlet.

———. *Scenic Byways: Preserving a Part of America's Heritage*. Pamphlet.

Schweitzer, Robert, and Michael W. R. Davis. *America's Favorite Homes: Mail-Order Catalogues as a Guide to Popular Early 20th Century Houses*. Detroit: Wayne State University Press, 1990.

Scimmel, Julie. "Inventing the Indian." In *The West as America: Reinterpreting Images of the Frontier*, edited by William H. Truettner, 149–89. Washington, D.C.: Smithsonian Institution Press, 1991.

Sculle, Keith A. "Frank Redford's Wigwam Village Chain." In *Roadside America: The Automobile in Design and Culture*, edited by Jan Jennings, 125–35. Ames: Iowa State University Press, 1990.

Seratt, Dorothy R. L., and Terri Ryburn-Lamont. *Historic and Architectural Resources of Route 66 through Illinois*. National Register of Historic Places Multiple Property Nomination Form. Washington, D. C.: National Park Service, 1997.

Shepherd, Shawn. "The Legacy of Route 66: Highways Always Have an Economic Impact, Positive and Negative: The Mother Road Transformed New Mexico." *New Mexico Business Journal*, September 1, 2001. www.nmbiz.com/issues/01/Sep%2001; page now discontinued.

Shepherd-Lanier, Claire. "Trading on Tradition: Mary Jane Colter and the

Romantic Appeal of Harvey House Architecture." *Journal of the Southwest*, Summer 1996, 165–70.

Sherrill, Martha. "'55 Cadillac on Route 66: Tour Guide to Tad Pierson's American Dream Safari." *Esquire*, August 1995, 36–37.

Shull, Carol D. "Creating a Partnership." *Cultural Resource Management* 16.2 (1993): 4–5.

Slotkin, Richard. *Gunfighter Nation: The Myth of the Frontier in the Twentieth-Century America*. New York: Harper Perennial, 1992.

Smith, Greg. "Route 66 Revisited: Preserving the Mother Road." *Society for Commercial Archeology News*, Winter 1999–2000, 3–5.

Snyder, Tom. *Route 66: Traveler's Guide and Roadside Companion*. New York: St. Martin's Press, 1990.

Steinbeck, John. *The Grapes of Wrath*. New York: Viking Press, 1939. Reprint. New York: Penguin Books, 1976.

Stewart, George. *U.S. 40: A Cross Section of the United States of America*. Boston: Houghton Mifflin Company, 1953.

Stilgoe, R. John. *Metropolitan Corridor: Railroads and the American Scene*. New Haven, CT: Yale University Press, 1983.

Stipe, Robert E. "The Next Twenty Years." In *The American Mosaic: Preserving a Nation's Heritage*, edited by Robert E. Stipe and Antoinette J. Lee, 266–92. Washington, D.C.: U.S. Committee/International Council on Monuments and Sites, 1987.

Summa Fruit International. Canned grape label for "Route 66 Table Grapes." Ca. 1960, author's collection.

Tanner, Helen Hornbeck. *The Settling of North America: The Atlas of the Great Migrations into North America from the Ice Age to the Present*. New York: Macmillan, 1995.

Taylor, Michael. Interview with author, Santa Fe, New Mexico, August 11, 2003.

Teague, Tom, Bob Waldmire, and Lon Haldeman. *Searching for 66*. 1st ed. Springfield, IL: Samizdat House, 1991.

———. *Searching for 66*. 2d ed. Springfield, IL: Samizdat House, 1996.

Tiner, Jeanne D. *Route 66: Mainstreet of America*. Mesa, AZ: Terrell Publishing, 1998.

Trachtenberg, Stanley. *The Postmodern Movement: A Handbook of Contemporary Innovation in the Arts*. Westport, CT: Greenwood Press, 1985.

Trailnet. http://www.trailnet.org

U.S. Bureau of Census. "Bureau of Census Report on Courts." *Tourist Court Journal*, September 1950, 12.

U.S. Bureau of Transportation Statistics. http://www.bts.gov/publications/national_transportation_statistics/2005/index.html.

U.S. Congress. Route 66 Corridor Preservation Act. Public Law 106-45, Historic Preservation 16 U.S. Code Vol. 461, H.R. 66 1999.

U.S. Department of Energy, Department of Environmental Management. http://web.em.doe.gov/timeline/the50s.html

U.S. Department of the Interior. *Special Resource Study: Route 66*. Washington, D. C.: National Park Service, 1995.

u-s-history.com. http://www.u-s-history.com/pages/h3706.html

Vale, Thomas R., and Geraldine R. Vale, *U.S. 40 Today: Thirty Years of Landscape Change in America*. Madison: University of Wisconsin Press, 1983.

Van Slyck, Abigail A. "Racial Stereotypes and the Southwest's Vernacular Architecture." In *Gender, Class, and Shelter*, Perspectives in Vernacular Architecture 5, edited by Elizabeth C. Crowley and Carter L. Hudgins, 95–108. Knoxville: University of Tennessee Press, 1995.

Venturi, Robert, Denise Scott Brown, and Steven Izenour. *Learning from Las Vegas*. Cambridge, MA: MIT Press, 1977.

———. Lecture. Association for Preservation Technology annual conference, Philadelphia, PA, October 2000.

Wade, Edwin L. "The Ethnic Market in the Southwest." In *Objects and Others: Essays on Material Culture*, edited by George W. Stocking Jr., 167–91. Madison: The University of Wisconsin Press, 1985.

Wallace, Michael. *Mickey Mouse History and Other Essays on American Memory*. Philadelphia: Temple University Press, 1996.

Wallis, Michael. *Route 66: The Mother Road*. New York: St. Martin's Press, 1990.

———. Lecture. Route 66 Expo, Amarillo, TX, October 2, 1998.

———. Lecture. Second Annual International Route 66 Roadie Gathering, Tucumcari, New Mexico, July 10–13, 2003.

———. "Route 66, the Mother Road." Lecture, Route 66 Expo, Shamrock, TX, October 2, 1998.

West, Carroll Van, ed. *Tennessee Encyclopedia of History and Culture*. Nashville: Tennessee Historical Society, 1998.

Whitman, Walt. *Leaves of Grass*. http://www.princeton.edu/~batke/logr/log_082.html.

Wiegle, Marta, and Peter White. *The Lore of New Mexico*. Albuquerque: University of New Mexico Press, 1988.

———. "Southwest Lures: Innocents Detoured, Incensed Determined." *Journal of the Southwest*, Winter 1990, 499–510.

Wigwam Motel. "About the Wigwam Village." http://hometown.aol.com/spoo-linooo/myhomepage/business.html.

Wilburn, Gary. "Routes of History: Recreational Use and Preservation of Historic Transportation Corridors." *Information* 38. Washington, D.C.: National Trust for Historic Preservation, 1985.

Wilson, Chris. *The Myth of Santa Fe: Creating a Modern Regional Tradition*. Albuquerque: University of New Mexico Press, 1997.

Wilson, Steve. "Two-Lane Vacation: Highway Trip along What Is Left of Route 66 in New Mexico and Arizona Reveals a Bygone Era." *Travel Holiday*, April 1998, 23–25.

Witzel, Michael Karl. *Route 66 Remembered*. Osceola, WI: Motorbooks International, 1996.

Wolfe, Tom. *From Bauhaus to Our House*. Toronto: McGraw Hill, 1981.

Work Progress Administration Writer's Program. *Oklahoma: A Guide to the Sooner State*. Washington, D.C.: WPA, 1941.

Worster, Donald. *Dust Bowl: The Southern Plains in the 1930s*. New York: Oxford University Press, 1979.

Yagoda, Ben. *Will Rogers: A Biography*. New York: Alfred A. Knopf, 1993.

Index

Model T (Ford), 28–29
Moore, Bob, 75–77
Moran, Thomas, 16
Morrison, Jim, 94
Motel of the Mysteries (Macaulay), 96
motels, design of, 49–50;
    development of, 41–42;
    proliferation of on Route 66, 49;
    regional themes of on Route 66,
    44
"Mother Road," 39
Muir, John, 14–15
Mystic Chords of Memory, The
    (Kammen), 82

Natha, Mohammed, 122
National Geographic, 15–16
National Old Trails Road Association,
    30–31
National Register of Historic Places,
    68, 115–18; listed sites on Route
    66, 68, 104, 118
National Route 66 Corridor
    Preservation Program, 70, 125
National Route 66 Federation,
    6, 72, 90
Native Americans, 12–14; as "noble
    savages," 12; romanticizing of, 12,
    15; stereotypes of on Route 66, 51
Navajo Motel, 42
New Mexico Museum of the Old
    West (near Moriarty, New
    Mexico), 56–57, 104
nostalgia, 74, 79–80, 82, 94–95;
    compared to the study of history,
    94–95

Okies, 37–40, 88, 130
On the Road (Kerouac), 81
Osage Indian Trail, 10
Ozark Court (Sullivan, Missouri),
    43–44

Payne, Andy, 35
Pew, Thomas, Jr., 67
Pig Hip Restaurant (Broadwell,
    Illinois), 120–21
Pontiac Trail, 31
postmodernism, 100–102
pueblo revival style architecture, 21,
    26–27; on Route 66, 54
Pyle, C. C., 35

Queenan's Trading Post (Elk City,
    Oklahoma), 51

railroad landscapes, 11
rail travel, 11
Redford, Frank, 44
Rittenhouse, Jack D., 48, 68
Rio Pecos Ranch Truck Terminal
    (Santa Rosa, New Mexico), 54
roads, development of, 29–30,
    32; federal involvement in, 31;
    highway shield, 33; numbering of
    highways, 33
roadside businesses, advertising
    of, 42; conflict with downtown
    businesses, 32–33; development
    of, 32
Rogers, Will, 25, 46
Roosevelt, Franklin Delano, 40
Roosevelt, Theodore, 24
Rosaldo, Renato, 13–14
Round Up Motel (Claremore,
    Oklahoma), 55
Route 66, accidents on, 40, 93–94;
    bypasses on, 41; compared to
    interstates, 97–98; dangers on,
    57; decreased traffic on, 60–61; as
    endangered, 103, 107–8; fan clubs
    for, 70–71; historical periods
    of, 34; historical significance
    of, 69; increased traffic on, 36,
    40–41, 48, 109; interpretation
    of, 123; as linear "amusement
    park," 89; New Deal's impact